Book 1 — Worst of Mothers ... Best of Moms

ROBERT DAY has dedicated his adult life to child welfare issues. Over those years, many have been moved by excerpts from his incredibly painful childhood. God has now opened the door for this full, gripping account, detailing Robert's struggle through poverty, rejection, hunger and abuse. *Worst of Mothers ... Best of Moms* will move you to tears, but will also inspire ... bringing you to your feet as you celebrate the wonder of God's endless grace.

— TIM CLINTON ED. D., AMERICAN ASSOCIATION
OF CHRISTIAN COUNSELORS PRESIDENT

I HAVE KNOWN Robert Day for a number of years and have been thoroughly impressed with his great love for ministry. He has had a profound impact on so many young people who have had the privilege of being blessed by his story. Now, we can all be blessed through his brand new book, *Worst of Mothers ... Best of Moms*. I encourage you to read it, ponder its message, and allow it to motivate you to serve God through serving others.

— JONATHAN FALWELL, PASTOR,
THOMAS ROAD BAPTIST CHURCH, LYNCHBURG, VA

Book 2 — Desperately Healed ... My Journey to Wholeness

IN TODAY'S WORLD with all the rhetoric concerning the "war on poverty" who better to lead that battle than Robert Jay Day. We have been friends for over 40 years, we've climbed those Appalachian mountains in eastern Kentucky and managed to walk away "more than conquerors." Robert's insight and personal life stories prove the Biblical truth "with God all things are possible." My prayer is that this book will move the reader to be "doers of the word and not hearers only." My challenge is for us all to honor God and be a blessing to others. It is my joy to call Robert my friend and my brother in Christ.

— MARVIN BROWN, IT ANALYST SENIOR, MOBILE AL

WITH THE STORIES recounted in his first book, I had difficulty reconciling the Robert Day I have come to know with the devastating childhood I was reading about. With a humble spirit, Robert makes it clear that only by God's grace has he walked where none would choose to walk, yet rather than wallow in despair, has soared to devote his life to helping children at risk of their own despair.

— DAVID MARSHALL, CHAIRMAN OF THE BOARD,
PATRICK HENRY FAMILY SERVICES

What Amazon customers said about *Worst of Mothers...Best of Moms*: Book 1 in the Rescuing Children – Healing Adult series.

THE AUTHOR CAPTURED my attention and I couldn't put this book down. A must read. Can't wait until his next book comes out!

HOW CAN YOU SAY you love a book that tells the story of such a devastating childhood, except that Robert J. Day has written his story with hope on every page. His story shocked and saddened me, but did not leave me hopeless. It left me with a resolve to care and get involved.

I AM AN AVID READER and found this to be one of those books you can't put down. *Worst of Mothers...Best of Moms* is inspiring, thoughtful and honest. Don't pass it up.

ONE OF THE MOST compelling books I've read in years!

I AM GLAD this author wrote this book and shared his story. Thank you!

MUCH OF MY READING is for inspiration and encouragement and this book speaks to both. True inspiration and encouragement comes from enduring some difficulties and Mr. Day captures that in the pages of this book. Parts are hard to read but it made me even more aware of the care-free, candy-coated life I have been blessed to lead. My eyes were opened to the reality of so many children around us today who suffer in unimaginable circumstances and are wounded for life, generation after generation.

A WONDERFUL MEMOIR on the resilience of child. Great reminder that even small acts of kindness can carry a child in abusive and neglected situations a long way.

THIS IS ONE of those rare books which cuts across genres and aptly demonstrates how biography is intricately entwined with social ideas and spiritual formation.... Those working in the field of alleviating poverty or wounded families will find the thread of story which often is submerged by cold statistics and data. Those who are interested in the triumph of the will over adversity and deprivation will be buoyed by the determination to overcome by one who previously put a gun in his mouth contemplating how to end his suffering.

A POIGNANT STORY about being born into poverty, not only physical but spiritual poverty.... I look forward with anticipation to the next book in his series.

Desperately
Healed ...
My Journey
TO *Wholeness*

ROBERT J. DAY, MSW, M.Div
CEO of Patrick Henry Family Services

On the cover: In 1982, Robert Day married the woman who would change his life, Karen Haynes. Through thick and thin they forged a marriage of healing, joy, and understanding. Having raised four amazing children, today they often take a moment or two to simply enjoy being with one another. Robert is the first to admit his wife of 34 years is a cornerstone in his life as outlined in *Desperately Healed ... My Journey to Wholeness*.

Published by
Patrick Henry Family Services Publishing
1621 Enterprise Drive
Lynchburg, VA 24502
434-239-6891
patrickhenry.org

Cover design by Richard McClintock
Interior design by Jon Marken, Lamp-Post Publicity
Editing by Jennifer Wall, David Marshall,
Myra Green, Richard McClintock, and Jon Marken
Marketing by Beckie Nix

Printed in the United States of America

ISBN: 978-0-9979026-2-4

Be who you needed when you were younger.

Unknown

Contents

Preface

THIS IS THE SECOND INSTALLMENT in a three-part series titled *Rescuing Children, Healing Adults*. In the first book, *Worst of Mothers...Best of Moms*, I recounted my troubled childhood and discussed ways the local church can make a difference for the population of children often referred to as "at-risk." In this book, I share how my childhood negatively affected my life as an adult and the different steps I took toward healing. In the first book I tried to answer the question, "How did you get out of that mess?" This time the goal is to answer a second frequently asked question, "How did you find healing?"

I must confess, it was far easier writing about my childhood. While it stirred up deep emotions, it wasn't difficult being transparent. After all, I was just a kid. I was the victim. This has been more of challenge. Being open about the mistakes I've made, and the hurt I've caused as an adult, was quite a bit harder to transpose for all to read. Any pain I felt in the process of recording this part of my story is the embarrassment of self-inflicted wounds.

This second in the series picks up where the first left off, with only a few reminders, or hints, of what occurred earlier. My intention is for it to stand alone as much as possible. Nevertheless, having the context of the first will undoubtedly make the second much more meaningful.

Also, like the first, this book is not meant to be a complete autobiography. I tell only enough of my story to illustrate the topic. It's also not a self-help book. I'm neither a trained psychologist nor a licensed therapist. Admittedly, my counseling skills are horrible. I'm just not wired that way. I do, however, have high regard for those who are. During my first pastorate I tried to provide counseling to my congregation and community. It was something I thought I should do. I abruptly quit after three clients basically told me I was the worst counselor they had ever known. So, I'm just telling my story, my way, with the sincere hope someone might find it helpful.

Please take the following for what it is, a humble attempt to make sense of my bumpy journey as an adult who suffered childhood trauma, and to give some friendly advice for those with similar backgrounds. I pray it may help others have a successful Second Act, despite the unfortunate setbacks of the first.

Introduction

MY SON GAVE THE FOLLOWING SPEECH at the September 16, 2016, launch of *Worst of Mothers…Best of Moms*, the first in the *Rescuing Children — Healing Adults* series.

I couldn't be more proud of my father. I was one of the many people who encouraged him to put his story in a book, not because it's entertaining or necessarily enjoyable, although it is thought-provoking and thoroughly engaging. It is not a unique story, nor does it have any ground-breaking ideas, but rather it is a story all too common and heartbreaking. It is uncomfortable. It pulls at the heartstrings, and it is a story full of shocking poverty, depravity, and disbelief.

However, in his story you will also find more than a kernel of hope, grace, and faithfulness. You will find instruction and motivation to do something — and that is why I am glad to see my father's story between binding — written down to help others.

To my father and mother's credit, my father's story is not my story. In fact, my story is frankly boring in comparison, but far less disturbing. And for that, I will always be thankful for godly Christian parents.

I did not inherit a family legacy of rejection, destitution, and sin, but rather one of godliness, prosperity, and love. Growing up, I did not know my father's full story. We would often hear bits and pieces of it, but they were more comical tales than sad. Now that I know the full story I have come to have a greater appreciation for my father and how he did not let the past shape his future in a negative way, but allowed it to fuel a passion to help children who share the same story.

This book, while it may motivate or enlighten its readers, to me it is family history—an explanation of who my father is and how he became the man he is today. Even more important, it is a reminder of God's grace that I have inherited a life of faith and not depravity, prosperity not poverty, and the love of a father influenced by his past—motivated by it—impassioned by it—informed by it—but not ruled by it.

My dad is an inspiration to me and I am glad he has shared his story with me and everyone. I hope he is as much of an inspiration to you as he is to me.

— Alec J. Day

As you can imagine, I was very proud of Alec, as well as humbled by his words. It pleased me to hear him say he did not suffer because of the lasting affects of trauma I experienced as a child. I tried my best to shield him, and his sisters, from the problems and pain of my past. Regrettably, I was in the midst of the healing process as he was growing up, and I feared my struggles negatively affected the whole family more than it should have.

Thoreau is often quoted as saying, "Most men live lives of quiet desperation." My desperation has not always been silent. The trauma of childhood abuse, the tenacious impact of poverty, and the pervasive influence of my fallen culture sometimes caused my inner despair to ooze out in inappropriate and unproductive ways. I should warn you, though, there's nothing salacious or scandalous in these pages: no prison, no drugs, no affairs. I managed to avoid the big dramatic kinds of things that destroy so many people's lives who share a background similar to mine. Perhaps, something can be learned from that.

1
Loved

"You wouldn't want to marry me ... would you?"

I MET THE MOST BEAUTIFUL and amazing woman at Cumberland College through my work with Mountain Outreach. The ministry put out a call for help after Lee Leforce died of complications from frostbite he got while sleeping in the deplorable structure he called home. She was one of many who responded, attending one of our weekly meetings to learn how to get involved. I'd seen her on campus a few times and was hoping for an opportunity to meet. She was on a list I had made of various girls I wanted to date. If that sounds a bit cocky, trust me, it wasn't. I didn't see myself as any kind of "ladies man." On the contrary, I had little confidence in that area of my life. I was on the hunt for a girlfriend because of deficits I had, not because of some assets I thought I possessed.

People who are not whole, or who are hurting emotionally, often seek romantic relationships to fill the void. They have an intense need to be loved, or at least to feel loved. It's never the answer, though, especially for the other person being used as a type of psychotropic medication to deaden the pain. The reason is rather obvious. Hurting people tend to hurt other people, especially the ones closest to them. Relationships built on this type of faulty foundation will usually end badly. When they do, of course, it only adds to their attachment injuries and sense of desperation. I think it's why my mother had so many failed relationships. Not only was she looking for love in all the wrong places, she was looking for love for all the wrong reasons. Throughout four marriages and countless other relationships, she never found it, nor did she ever learn how to give it.

Since I didn't know the young lady on my list, she was simply recorded as "cute girl in green pants." When I saw her at the meeting, I quickly went into action. I asked her name, and after a bit of chit-chat, asked her out. Someone must have tripled-dog-dared her, because she agreed. WOW!

The following night I was to pick her up at her dorm, but David Emmert, my roommate and co-founder of Mountain Outreach, reminded me it was my turn to check on Lee's intellectually disabled son Arthur. This was just days after Lee had died, and a few volunteers were taking turns going to his shack daily until we found a facility willing to take him. Since it was winter, we would bring in firewood, stoke the fire, and give him something to eat. I asked David if he would take my turn, but he also had plans. He did, however, let me borrow his truck.

My date was born in Rhode Island, but grew up surrounded by the majestic mountains and ocean inlets of Southeast Alaska. Karen Haynes was raised in the middle of a middle-class family where church, education, and work were valued. She had chosen to attend a college in the "lower 48," and because of her long fascination with horses, picked Kentucky. Sadly for her, happily for me, she went to the wrong part of the state for that. Her major was Early Childhood Education with an emphasis in Special Education. We had very little in common.

It was North meets South, good student meets bad, rational and logical meets unpredictable and emotional. Yet our birthdays were only three days apart. We were both introverts. We shared a common faith, felt called to serve others, and thought the other was pretty unique. We were also two lonely individuals, not necessarily a solid basis for a long-term relationship. The source of her sense of isolation was geographical. She was a long way from her family. Mine was cultural distance. I was a long way from how I was raised.

Karen had never seen poverty like what was in the mountains of Kentucky, but she experienced it firsthand that evening. I told her I needed to go by and check on a friend on our way to the movies. That was all right with her. I didn't explain anything to her before we got there, and didn't give a second thought how this might appear to her. If it had been a horror film, the audience would have been yelling, "Don't go in in there!"

After parking at the end of a dirt road, stepping onto slippery rocks to cross a creek, and walking as carefully as we could through the muck of a wintery field so as not to mess up our nice date clothes, we finally arrived at Lee's dilapidated, unlit house just as it was getting dark. I knocked. Arthur came to the door completely naked from head to toe. I told him to get back inside and put on some clothes. He ran back to the filthy mattress he lay on day and night and jumped under the tattered covers. I fiddled with the fire and got some additional wood while he ate something I snuck from the college cafeteria. Since there was no desirable place to sit, Karen stood and watched in silence.

After we finished, we headed back to the truck. About halfway through the muddy field, it dawned on me what I had just put her through. It also struck me that the petite, pretty girl who was walking beside me did not once flinch, gag, or even gasp at the revolting sights, sounds, and smells of the darkened dwelling. That very moment, I decided I was going to marry her. Later in my dorm room, after dessert at Shoney's Big Boy [with this astonishing woman], I tore up my list.

That was a Friday. I asked Karen to marry me on Sunday while eating at Pizza Hut on our second outing. Just as she was taking a bite of ham and pineapple pizza (still our favorite), I awkwardly proposed, "You wouldn't want to marry me...would you?" Without hesitation she said, "Yes." Actually, I think she just nodded her head, but she swears to this day she verbalized it.

I had spent all the money I had in the world on those two dates with Karen. Not knowing when, or even if, I could ever afford a third, and realizing what a gem she was, I decided to "lock her in" before anyone else had a chance. I skipped the girlfriend stage and went straight for the binding nature of an engagement. Other than the commitment to follow Christ, it has been the best decision I have ever made, albeit a bit hasty.

Looking at it now, it was a crazy thing to do. As a father, I see it from a completely different viewpoint today. We both recognize it could have been the biggest mistake of our lives. Fortunately, someone was looking out for us. Mamma Joyce (one of my substitute mothers) insisted we wait. Her stern motherly advice convinced us to make sure this was right before we made such a critical life decision.

There are so many young people desperately wanting someone to love them. Attempting to quiet the demands of their inner anguish, they make rash decisions that negatively affect the direction and quality of their lives. If they don't get this part right coming out of the gate, they'll most likely just be adding insult to injury. Even worse, the children conceived from those needy associations will likely suffer as well, and the disastrous cycle will repeat itself.

Karen and I went to premarital counseling, something we highly recommend to everyone thinking about getting married. We took a compatibility test and read a couple of books on the subject of building a successful marriage. After one year of engagement, and with the blessing of Mamma Joyce, we were married during Christmas break, December 20th, 1982. We were both barely 21. We held the service in Corbin, Kentucky (birthplace of Kentucky Fried Chicken) at Calvary Baptist Church, where I was serving as a part-time youth minister. I think the whole thing cost less than one hundred dollars.

My mentor, Vic Edwards, who had talked me into going to college and pulled strings to get me in, performed the ceremony. David Emmert was one of my groomsmen. Marvin Brown, another roommate and old friend from the days when I lived in the two-story trailer, was my best man. If I hadn't sat behind Marvin in ninth grade math class, where I could see his answers (unbeknownst to him), I wouldn't have passed. Marvin has his own story of overcoming great obstacles to succeed. Maybe one day he will tell it.

---

494. The Wedding Vow

I love my wife. When I say "my wife," it's not the same as saying "my car" or "my house." It's not even the same as saying "my life." She's not my possession. My wife is not some object I may love one minute and curse the next. My love for her is not some fleeting feeling. She's my wife because I'm her husband. The symbiotic relationship is not equal to any kind of object or person on earth.

The kind of love my wife and I share is fully realized in the words of the wedding vow: "To love and to cherish, in sickness or in health, and forsaking all others, to cleave to one another for as long as we both shall live."

This vow speaks of a commitment to one another that's found only in marriage. It's a commitment to love always. We will love each other when we are at our best. We will love each other when we are at our worst. There's simply no other option.

StraightTalkwithRobertDay.org

The first time I met Karen's parents, they came down from Alaska just a couple of days before the wedding. Karen's father and I waited in Karen's apartment while she and her mother were doing "wedding stuff." They thought we fellows needed time to bond. Conversation was awkward, however. I tried to strike up a dialogue on a number of different topics, but nothing was clicking. We had absolutely nothing in common, except we both loved Karen.

Someone came to the door selling Peanut Brittle for a fundraiser at a dollar a box. I thought it was a chance to impress my future father-in-law with what a nice guy I was, so I bought a box. After I managed to find a dollar and pay the guy, I turned around expecting affirmation of my generous character, but instead he scolded, "I hope you're not going to waste money like that when you're married to my daughter." I laughed. I thought he was joking. He wasn't. For several Christmases after we were married, I gave him a box of Peanut Brittle as a gift. He still doesn't think it's funny. By the way, my father-in-law's fear was warranted. I wasted a lot of money in my life, but not by giving it to charity. In my opinion, it is never a waste of money to help people.

After becoming husband and wife, we continued going to school, volunteered in Mountain Outreach, and played Ultimate Frisbee when we could find the time. We grew together as a couple in our tiny basement apartment with the leaky bathtub faucet and abundance of water bugs. We were probably poorer than the average married college couple. Our rent was only $75 a month, but that was usually a challenge. We had a dining room table with no chairs, so we ate our meals on our "couch of many colors" given to us by Mountain Outreach. It was so ugly and worn they couldn't give it away to anybody else. We drank from an odd assortment of yard sale glasses and used mason jars. We had very little, but we were happy, and happy was enough for us.

Karen has been by my side ever since that mission date to Lee's house. I'm not sure where I first read or heard it, but it's true: a happy marriage is one in which each person thinks they got a better partner than they deserve. I definitely got better than I deserved. She no longer has those green pants, but they'd still fit if she did. She does still have the same alluring green eyes I saw the day I fell in love with her. She's no longer cute, though. She is beautiful!

Despite being on the short end of the stick, Karen has stuck with me in sickness and health, for richer and poorer (haven't see the richer part yet), in good times and bad. We have been blessed with four wonderful children and a rewarding life of service to God. It's so very much more than I ever conceived possible or ever dared hoped for my life. However, it almost didn't happen. The first time Karen saw me she was not impressed. In fact, she thought I was a "big jerk."

One of the requirements at Cumberland College was attending weekly chapel. They didn't have many good speakers in those days and a lot of us students resented going, and often didn't. They only reason we did at all was because they gave a grade for attendance. I actually failed chapel the second semester of my freshman year. It was the only F grade on my college transcript. That would later haunt me when I prepared to graduate and learned I was a quarter of a point short of getting my diploma. Thankfully, the administration thought my years of service in Mountain Outreach, where we had built fifteen homes for the poor, was at least equivalent to a semester of chapel.

One of the bad speakers they had during my chapel "protest" semester was me.

It was tradition back then for school officials to invite a couple of ministerial students to deliver the message. We were called the "preacher boys." Since I was on that track, and because I already had some preaching experience, they gave me the opportunity to address my fellow students. It was quite an honor for a freshman. I'm pretty sure they regretted it. First of all, my style that fit so well in country churches wasn't so appropriate in that academic setting. Secondly, the content of my messages in those days was gleaned from my own uneducated study of the Scriptures. Thirdly, I was a bold idealist in those days (still am I guess) and I didn't mind making people uncomfortable. In fact, I thought that was my job. And lastly, I was a confused, troubled, and hurting kid who had no business with such an important responsibility.

Overconfidence is the most dangerous form of carelessness. I wasn't cocky in front of the opposite sex, but I certainly was behind the pulpit. I began my scantily prepared sermon by asking all of the Christians in the Gatliff Auditorium to stand. They nervously complied. Then I told them to look at the lost, unsaved people sitting around them. "Go on, take a good look," I demanded. "They are going to hell and it's your fault." Yes, I actually said that. After they sat back down, I went on to tell them about one of my uncles getting stabbed to death in bar fight, and how I was pretty sure he was in hell because no one told him about Jesus.

My uncle Buddy was a Vietnam vet. He labored hard at low-paying jobs to support his family. His lifestyle of drinking, and the pervasive culture around him that encouraged violence to solve conflict, led to his tragic demise at the D&M Tavern, known to the locals as the Devil's Mansion. I will always remember my uncle, though, for one single act of kindness. One Christmas, while living with my Grandmother Wood, he gave me the only gift I received—a cheap flashlight from the Dollar General Store. It wasn't the gift but the thoughtfulness that I remember so fondly.

I passionately ranted on for thirty minutes as my peers looked on with bewilderment. My message was a combination of emotional vomit and an incoherent proclamation of the saving power of Jesus Christ. I'm still ashamed when I think about it now. Emotionally unhealthy people will often subconsciously take out their pain on others who had nothing to do with it. Religious people wield the additional weapons of God and the Bible to transmit their torment to others. There are many unhealthy churches led by broken individuals who have never been healed from their trauma. I know because I was one of them. I will tell you more about that later. Nonetheless, churches seldom ask questions about past abuse or trauma when looking for their spiritual leaders. They certainly should.

My future bride was in the audience that day. After we were engaged, she told me how I had embarrassed and angered her.

I'm certain she wasn't alone in her feelings. However, here is the amazing thing about that foolish sermon. I gave an evangelistic invitation at the end of my message (something rarely done at that Christian school), and about a half-dozen students came forward and prayed to receive Jesus Christ as their Lord and Savior.

That wouldn't be the last time I did the right thing, the wrong way. Despite the popular meme, good intention is rarely ever good enough. Happily, I got to redeem myself when they gave me another chance my senior year. I can't remember what I preached, but I do recall being more prepared, balanced, articulate, but still challenging. It was enthusiastically received by students and faculty alike. It reflected I was in a better place emotionally, and that my education was having some positive effect.

I wish I could say I never embarrassed or angered Karen again by a sermon I delivered, or by something I did in the "service of God." I cannot. There was a great deal of growing up and changing I needed to do. My precious wife patiently and lovingly carried the weight of our marriage and family life until I got to that place. It's safe to say that women, in general, tend to be more mature than the men they marry, and they have to spend a great deal of time domesticating the men in their lives. However, Karen had more than the usual burden. I brought a wealth of poverty and an abundance of needs to the sacred union. There's no doubt, she married a fixer-upper.

The most challenging part of rescuing at-risk children is when they become adults. They can have an extremely difficult time breaking the negative patterns they learned from their dysfunctional family or destructive culture. Research is showing that trauma from abuse, and even from poverty itself, can actually change the way the brain works. Distressed children can form new "norms" in their thought process, which then determines their behavior. At Patrick Henry Family Services, we view the children in our care from the perspective of "What has happened to this child?" instead of "What is wrong with this child?" That does not absolve them of bad conduct. It only provides a reason behind it. I believe it's a more grace-filled approach to working with children and adults dealing with pattern-controlled behaviors. Consider the contrast between the approach of legalism and grace. Notice how each addresses an individual caught in those kinds of negative actions.

Legalism demands — stop being a perpetrator of sin.

Grace pleads — stop being a casualty of sin.

Note: Recognizing you are a victim of sin, and not merely a perpetrator of it, does not give license to play the victim card. Claiming injured status, while worshipping the Savior who died for our sin, is a type of sin itself. Please stop. You won't get better until you do.

The period of our lives when we have to do the most transformational work, which is generally in our roaring twenties, is usually when these vulnerable adults are abandoned by the system and have the fewest resources. Because they have little to no support, they have to figure it all out on their own, or at best, with other similarly deprived peers. Many never do. Helping children means nothing in the end if we can't support their transition into becoming decent adults.

Without help and healing, children coming from hard places become hardened adults. Hardened adults often raise children in hard places. Hurt begets Hard. Hard begets Hurt. Without intervention, the cycle will repeat itself for infinity.

Just like many of the emerging adults we serve at Patrick Henry Family Services through our Step Forward program, I had to overcome a number of barriers to become responsible. Certain beliefs and attitudes obtained in my childhood negatively affected my life as an adult. It wasn't merely a matter of maturity. Here are just a few examples:

Not showing up to work because I didn't feel like going, and then getting fired.

Leaving a job before I had another.

Buying an expensive television when we didn't have the money to pay all the bills.

Moving from one state to another without knowing where we were going to live, or how.

Living by the philosophy: good enough is more than enough.

I'm not proud of those things. They were bad decisions and they caused my family needless stress and unnecessary anxiety. I share them now to demonstrate some of the challenges those coming out of poverty and dysfunction face as they move from childhood to adulthood. Sometimes they don't make it. They stay stuck in their old destructive patterns. Yet we falsely assume because they're now adults, they should know better and act wiser. They are quickly written off as unredeemable, which in turn creates a self-fulling prophecy where they become what they are labeled.

"You can take the boy out of the mountains but you can never take the mountains out of the boy."

I've heard that many times. It's a polite way of saying what I've heard growing up about my family of origin. "You can't wash trash from white trash." While I hope all the best parts of mountain culture remain a part of my identity, I'm living proof a person can significantly change for the good. It is actually possible to get the mountains out of the boy, and it's especially desirable if the mountains get in the boy's way of living a healthy and productive life. That idea gives new meaning to the words of Jesus when he said, and I paraphrase, "If you have faith the size of a mustard seed, you can tell that mountain to get up and get out of your way."

Poor people have poor ways because poverty has a way of degrading the mind and trashing the soul. Education was a huge part of my transformational journey. The education process, more than the product, moved me from a culture of poverty to a thoroughly middle-class life. The true evil of poverty isn't its lack of resources, or even the suffering of its depravity, but rather the lies it tells those trapped in it. Education didn't just provide diplomas that could be leveraged for better job opportunities. It did something much more profound. It changed the size and scope of my world. Poverty, like fear, distorts perception. The power of education is its ability to change perception, to alter what is possible. I'm a firm believer that a person can change their life by simply changing the way they think (see Appendix B), which isn't actually that easy; simple, yes, easy, no. Education is the vehicle that makes it even possible.

What's at stake if we don't fix the poverty problem? Why should those who are not poor care about those who are?

It's about the kids. It's not about feeling sorry for them, or about some sense of social injustice. It's certainly not because they don't have as much stuff as rich kids do. It is more a practical matter. Poverty damages children. That's the bottom line. They are traumatized, not so much by lack of income, but by all the other things associated with poverty. As a matter of national interest, we should all be concerned because children of poverty become adults of poverty, and it's costing us not only our treasure but also our talent.

Did you know that children who are exposed to poverty at a young age have trouble academically later in life? But it's even worse than that. According to research, poverty appears to be associated with smaller brain volumes in areas involved in emotion processing and memory. That's just one of the many reasons why we must fix the poverty problem.

Despite all the academic study, and billions in government spending on the War on Poverty, preventing poverty while living in a free and rich society is really quite simple. It's also a great deal cheaper than what we've been led to believe. Statistics inform us that if individuals simply make four critical decisions they are nearly guaranteed not to be poor in America.

1. Stay in school and graduate. Data shows education increases the chance of prosperity. Finishing high school is a must. Some additional education after that improves the odds even more.

2. When you do have children, be certain you are in a committed,

long-term, stable relationship. Single parenthood is one of the leading causes of poverty, especially households headed by women. Marriage is a powerful poverty repellent.

3. Postpone having children until you have gainful employment. Studies continue to show the beneficial effects for both parent and child. It's just common sense.

4. Stay away from addictive substances of every kind. They can easily destroy all the gains made by the first three wise decisions.

With the encouragement of others, I did all four of those crucial tasks and my life has been blessed because of it. Every member of my birth family, with only two exceptions, did just the opposite and the consequences are consistent with the statistics. However, for people raised in a culture of poverty, doing those four simple things may be the toughest decisions they'll ever make.

The common denominator for all four of these important life choices is the ability to delay gratification—to put off until later what is wanted today. Unfortunately, in a free and rich society, where the social safety net softens the blows of poor decision making, it's one of the hardest things a person has to master. If we can teach young people to say no, and train them to wait, we can keep them from the poorhouse and dramatically improve the quality of their lives, and consequently, the lives of their children.

In addition to poverty, pornography was one particularly vile problem I had to overcome. It took a hidden toll the early years of our marriage. Anyone who knows my story can understand why it was a struggle. In addition to going through puberty and adolescence during the decade of the Sexual Revolution, my "real" father introduced me to hard core porn at age eleven. My mother fed me a steady diet of it throughout my teens. The first full book I ever read, besides *Run Dog Run*, was a pornographic novel. When I was twelve, the uncle for whom I'm named taught me how to use "dirty magazines" for personal pleasure, when we shared that ghastly attic bedroom together. Sometimes we did it with other kinfolk (male and female) all sharing the same bed. Incest took various forms in my birth family. I was also sexually abused by a pastor and sexually exploited by a doctor. None of those experiences justify it, by any means, but they do provide some reason for it.

It was in the middle of my first pastorate when I finally dealt with it in any serious way. I knew it was wrong. I could see how it was destructive. I felt guilty about it…all the time. However, it wasn't until a night of prayer with a friend who had the same issue, followed by a time of fasting, that I began to get freedom from its grip. Up to that point I had kept my secret from Karen, although I'm certain my porn problem often caused her discomfort and shame without her fully understanding its source.

I felt a confession to her, and my congregation, would be a necessary part of my trek toward wholeness and would provide much-needed accountability. The darkness had to be exposed to the light. It was painful to tell her. It was more painful for her to hear it.

When dealing with wounded people, we need to be mindful they are often chained, like prisoners, to their gnawing troubles. Their history blackmails them. It's added insurance they'll keep the secret to themselves. It's only when they are brave enough to expose the past, and its dirty secrets, that they can start down the road to real recovery.

After that, things progressively got better. The temptation remained to a smaller degree. Occasionally I would slip and give into its carnal lure. But it was different. It was now something that came at me from outside myself, whereas before it had come from deep within me. There was a clear connection between my feelings of rejection and that singularly ungodly urge. From early adolescence, porn had been my self-medication to combat feelings of loneliness and depression. It had become my spiritual stronghold. Yet, as the Lord granted me control over those worthless feelings, the power of porn lessened considerably.

As it did, I started seeing my wife through more sanctified eyes and began wondering if I'd even loved her when we were first married. I'm sure I did at some level, but after a decade of marriage I felt it necessary to commit to her from a position of strength instead of weakness. So for our eleventh wedding anniversary I decided to marry her again, although I didn't tell her.

I got her to the church on false pretenses where a gorgeous handmade wedding dress was waiting. I will always be grateful to Jodie Buck for the countless hours she spent on it. Some of the women from the congregation were there to do her hair and makeup. Our five-year-old son, dressed as my best man, said, "Dad wants to know if you will marry him again." She said yes, or so I was told. She may have just nodded again. An hour or so later we exchanged vows in the crowded sanctuary. This time it cost more than a hundred dollars and the reception was what it should have been the first time we did it. Our three-year-old daughter was her maid of honor. We went on a one-night honeymoon with our one-year-old daughter, I might add, because she was still breast feeding. It was a very special day.

Some are sent to foreign fields. Others to unique people groups. Some are called to meet a particular need or fight for a certain cause. Karen has been the missionary to my life. She has served as my angel-spouse — above me, pulling me upwards toward a higher calling. The metamorphosis into the person I am today is largely due to her. She has been partly my mother, partly my friend, partly my lover, and always my faithful partner. Karen has never allowed me to feel sorry for myself, nor has she ever let me settle for "good enough." Her steady presence in my life has been the anchor of security I needed to peel away the pain of my past and to become a better person. While I often worried she would leave me (a history of rejection denied me security in the relationship for a long time), and she might have had good cause, she never raised the white flag above her door. I wake up every day, look at her and say to myself, "Thank God she hasn't left me yet."

Marrying well was my first essential step to healing and normalcy. Learning to become a good father was the second. Although I was unaware of it at the time, my children (Alec, Naomi, Faith, and Sharon) played an existential role in my transformation. I swore a vow early on they would never experience what I did growing up, and they haven't. They were my motivation to grow and change. They are, in many ways, better people than I was at their age. There is little doubt in my mind that they've done more for me than I have done for them.

Mama Joyce once told Karen and me that raising healthy, balanced, and considerate children, who walk with God, would be the best gift we could give to the world. It would outweigh anything we did in His name and everything we did for others. She was right, as usual. At the time, though, I had no clue how to do that. I'd never seen it done.

The third night after the birth of my first child, I was overwhelmed with my new role as a father. My son was crying, my wife was exhausted, and my twenty-four-year-old inexperienced self was trying to get him to sleep. As I rocked him, physically weary and emotionally drained, I suddenly panicked at the realization of being responsible for this child for the next two decades.

I grew up with many men in my life from my mother's numerous failed relationships, but I never really had a father. Now, there I was with this precious, helpless infant and I had no idea how I was going to be his daddy. I did the only thing I knew to do. I drew on the only assistance available—I prayed to my Heavenly Father. Crying as much as my baby boy, I asked the Lord's help getting him to sleep, and for the wisdom and courage to raise him right. My Eternal Father faithfully answered both of my desperate pleas.

Here's the thing about children. They will make you a better person if you let them. It isn't the reason you should have them, but if you fully commit to your role as parent, it will radically change you. I learned something about myself and got better with each developmental stage my children went through—as if I was filling in missing pieces of my life through them. Each one also had their own special ability to push certain emotional buttons, which often forced me to take a hard look at my past. However, it was in their teens that I had an epiphany. It would become the building block for all the rest of my reconstruction into a new creature.

As my children were growing and getting to the point where they were embarrassed for me to say "I love you" in public, I found a way to communicate those reassuring words without actually saying them. As I dropped them off at school, or some activity where their peers were present, I would look them in the eye and simply say "remember." They would nod or say, "I will."

I wanted my children to remember I loved them and that they should never, ever, doubt it. That simple single word, and the knowledge that it was true, provided them with security and confidence as they launched out further and further from my presence. They could fail or mess up, but it would be okay because my love for them would always be unconditional. It also served to keep them from temptation. I knew my children would inevitably be drawn to do something they shouldn't. It was at those times I especially wanted them to remember they were loved.

Learning to love my children without question, I awakened to the realization I was loved the same way, yet perfectly, by my Heavenly Father. It put me in a spiritual place where I could see my past through a more hopeful lens. I could see I had always been loved, even when I was rejected, abused, and alone. My Eternal Father was with me through it all. It was my children who taught me that lesson.

Bottom line: For healing and wholeness to take place, one must be loved unconditionally, and then learn to love others the same way.

2
Delivered

I had to get free to learn, so I could learn to be free.

UNBEKNOWNST TO ME AT THE TIME, I became a casualty in the "battle for the Bible" during my years in college. The wounds inflicted from that doctrinal fight arrested my spiritual growth and hampered my healing, for a time.

I was 17 in 1978 when I became a Christian and joined the ranks of the Southern Baptists, who had been gripped with the issue of biblical inerrancy for much of the decade. The good people at Newcomb Baptist Church believed and taught the simple meaning of the Scriptures. They didn't always live by it, but they never denied its authority in their lives. As far as they were concerned, if the Bible said it, they believed it, and that settled it. They may have been hypocrites at times (as are all believers), but they were never unbelievers. To use a thought from the poet Matthew Arnold, their vice paid tribute to their virtue.

The bought-by-the-blood, bond-by-the-Bible, born-again, baptized believers in my home church judiciously warned me the college I attended, a Southern Baptist institution, would "ruin me." They were right.

I went to Cumberland College fully confident in the Scriptures I preached. I had never questioned The Word. There was never any reason. I was unequipped to deal with the various controversies and conflicts brought on by academia's love of biblical criticism, as well as the developing postmodern distrust of all things grounded in historical authority. It certainly didn't help that I was a bad student. I could barely read, let alone understand the sundry arguments of ivory tower scholars. Plus, I trusted my professors. They were authorities who were supposed to know what they were talking about. Right? In rather short order, I traded in preaching the gospel to win lost souls for the "greater good" of a social gospel. I still loved God with all my heart, and earnestly desired to help others, but those righteous affections got translated into building homes, instead of pastoring people, as I had originally surrendered my life to do.

---

477. The Unbelievable

The value of Christianity lies precisely in that it is not always rational, philosophical, or external. Its usefulness lies in the unforeseen, the miraculous, and the extraordinary.

Christianity, as opposed to the philosophies of man, attracts reckless devotion because it demands absolute faith. The philosopher and the scientist aspire to explain away all mysteries, to dissolve them into the light of human reason. It is natural for the natural man to attempt to put all things in a test tube so he can observe, explain, and control all things. But Christianity, on the other hand, demands and passionately pursues the mysterious. In fact, it is the unknown of the supernatural, not the predictability of the natural, that constitutes the very essence of worship.

The first verse of chapter one in the book of Hebrews explains it well: Christian faith is the substance of things hoped for, and the convictions of things not seen. In other words, the value of Christian faith is that it believes the unbelievable.

StraightTalkwithRobertDay.org

Looking back, I do not regret any of the work I did for the poor. It is as scriptural as evangelism, and there shouldn't be an ultimatum to choose between the two. We can do both. We should do both. We must do both. Like so many things God's children fight about, it's a false dichotomy, and you know what false dichotomies create? Bad decisions. To waste valuable resources arguing over which of the two is the true calling of the Christian is asinine. It's a forced choice between two half-truths. On this, and so many other issues, we need the power and genius of "and," instead of the weak and limited perspective of "or." There are a great deal more *ands* than *ors* in the Bible.

For me at the time, though, helping the poverty-stricken mountain folk was a way I "worked out my own salvation with fear and trembling." It was a type of therapy, a dynamic form of self-discovery. I probably got more out of helping the poor than the poor ever got from my helping them. Isn't that just like the Lord? He helps us by having us help others. It's a method that is as efficient as it is effective.

While I have often clashed with certain progressive elements of the profession, I don't regret getting a Social Work degree. I'm quite proud of that. Many of the skills I learned have served me well in so many areas, especially where I am now. I do, though, very much regret losing faith in the Scriptures. It was a waste of valuable years, because it was only when my faith was restored in God's Word that deep and lasting healing finally started taking place in my life.

I graduated from high school and college, a man with an education. It would take five years and two master's degrees before I truly became an educated man. Through college, I simply completed the minimum necessary to get a grade. In truth, I often didn't even do that. School, to me, was not about getting an education. It was about safety and having a social life. Certainly I learned a thing or two in high school and college, but it was outside the classroom I received the most benefit. Graduate school proved to be something entirely different.

After Cumberland, Karen and I moved to Louisville (properly pronounced Luvulle) Kentucky where I attended "The" Southern Baptist Theological Seminary and earned a degree in Social Work. A dozen years later we returned so I could get a Master of Divinity degree: not too bad for someone from a family, and a culture, that had little respect for education. At first I struggled, though. I did not have strong classroom skills. My usual bag of tricks, which had gotten me that far, didn't work so well at that scholastic level. I wasn't sure I'd make it.

The academic demands were far beyond my limited means. I didn't have a good grasp of the English language. I didn't understand how a verb worked in my native tongue, let alone in Greek or Hebrew. I still have problems mixing my tenses to this day. Reading was slow and laborious. Writing was torture. Punctuation, what's that? Additionally, I had no clue how to research a topic or write a proper paper. The only thing going for me was the fact I'm an auditory learner. If it was something presented in a lecture or discussed in class, I could usually remember it. God blessed me with a gift that helped tremendously throughout my life — the ability to learn by absorption. I just couldn't put anything I knew in writing in any manner that resembled an academic paper.

Then one day it all began to change. I got back a lengthy written assignment. The professor had bled red ink all over it. At the bottom of the last page, where there should have been a grade, there was a note, "Please make an appointment to see me." I nearly broke out in tears. I wanted to do well but just had too many deficits.

In his office, my professor went over the paper's many flaws. I tried to listen, but my mind rushed ahead to what seemed like the natural conclusion — failure — expulsion — shame. Yet to my surprise, he made a comment I'll always remember. "Robert, you have a keen mind. You have great ideas and a unique way of looking at an issue. You just need to learn how to express it properly." What? I have a keen mind? No one had ever told me that. Ever. From that day forward, I approached my studies as someone who could learn. I've been in control of my learning ever since.

Many poor people never break out of their poverty because they are convinced they're deficient in some way. They think of themselves as dumb. The poor are easily labeled as unteachable, and they readily accept it as true. It's likely they weren't educated well, but that's an entirely different matter than having some type of learning disability. We know that poverty does have a negative effect on IQ. The proof is clear. The stresses of poverty consume so much energy that they reduce cognitive function. However, the evidence also demonstrates IQ can improve in time, under the right circumstances. It's most likely, though, to improve in childhood and adolescence, and that's why good, quality education is an absolute must in our fight against poverty. Nevertheless, it's never too late to learn.

Regrettably, many poor people remain captive under the false narrative that they can't learn. Even if they could get past the cultural barriers, their personal limitations are ever present. Not only does this faulty paradigm keep them trapped in their poverty, it also serves to anchor them securely to the hurts and pains often connected with that poverty. Knowledge to overcome those problems is available but not readily accessible.

Let's be absolutely clear on this point: there is no healing, no transformation, no growth, no positive change of any kind, without learning. None. There is no teaching, only learning, and there will be no learning if you believe you can't, or shouldn't. By God's grace, I was delivered from both those terrible lies, and that is absolutely prerequisite to wellness. That goes for every socioeconomic status.

Of course, the changes wrought by both education and family have been firmly set in the context of a personal faith in a loving Heavenly Father. My spiritual formation has been the fuel that's powered my conversion from an abused child of poverty to a caring useful adult. For that to have come about, I had to first conquer my doubts about the Scriptures. Once I was convinced I could learn, I began studying the issue for myself. Oddly enough, it was while working on my social work degree I began to regain trust in the authority of the Scriptures, and consequently the power of God.

The most memorable, if not most controversial, sermon in the history of the Southern Baptist Theological Seminary was delivered the semester before I matriculated there. At the beginning of the fall semester of 1984, in a now famous convocation address, President Roy Honeycutt declared "holy war" against the "fundamentalists" who were attempting a takeover of the flagship institution. The sermon sent shockwaves throughout the entire denomination and made my time at Southern very interesting. I had gone to a theological seminary to learn church-based social work (the first and only one of its kind at the time), but I couldn't help getting caught up in the theological fray. Ultimately I decided I would decide for myself. I commenced studying the Bible in earnest, really for the first time in my life. I wanted to carefully examine the thing being criticized, rather than take the word of those who were doing the criticizing, or even of those defending the criticism. It's an important life lesson. It should be used in every area of life from doctrine, to politics, to consumer purchases, to what we hear about others.

Basically, I had to get free to learn so I could learn to be free. It didn't happen overnight, and it didn't occur in a vacuum. It was a journey, a journey I'm still on, although thankfully closer to the end than the beginning.

Of this, I am convinced: all problems are theological. Whether they be personal, or social, or political, all problems are the result of bad theology—of believing the wrong things. Submitting to the Bible's authority allows for a spiritual deliverance of every human hurt. Biblical truth, in the hands of the Holy Counselor, is powerful tonic. Prayer and fasting are tools that give aid to this kind of divine medicine. The Lord is in the business of transforming us from one degree of glory to the next. His desire is for us to become new creations. Unresolved wounds, pain from past experiences, out-of-control emotions, unproductive behaviors, addictions, and destructive thoughts have no place in a new creation. Those old things must pass away (not ignored or suppressed) in order for new things to surface. Being healed, and becoming spiritually mature (sanctified), are not mutually exclusive of the other. One does not manifest without the other. A good discipleship program could be just as helpful in the healing process (or solving social problems) as anything else I'll discuss in this book.

Think of it this way: growing is a form of healing. To be mature, we must first be healed of our immaturity. To overcome ignorance, we must obtain knowledge. That makes education a type of healing. In order to fully love and accept those who are different than us, we must be cured of our bigotry. Courage is the fix for fear. Foolishness is treated with wisdom. Get the point? Healing is growing. Growing is healing.

The kind of healing we are talking about here is predicated on forging a new identity in Christ. Fashioning that identity from a painful past is nothing less than miraculous, because there is not any damage in that identity, only health.

Just days before my thirty-first birthday, I found a level of spiritual mitigation from pornography, using nothing more than biblical truths and spiritual tools. On October 6th, 1992, on the twenty-second day of a forty-day time of prayer with some fasting, I wrote this journal entry:

David W. and I spent the late Wednesday evening and early Thursday morning hours in prayer for the destruction of strongholds in our lives. It was an intense time of prayer, praise, and cleansing. We began with a time of worship, then prayed that anger, lies, and pride be revealed for repentance. During this time I felt the very presence of God. My body began to tingle with a very pleasant sensation. We rebuked Satan and then asked the Holy Spirit to reveal times, through memories, where the roots of the stronghold of lust began.... David prayed and guided me through my past. The Spirit revealed one memory after another. I prayed for forgiveness for the people involved. I prayed to break the binds Satan had on me because of these incidents. Then I pleaded the blood of Jesus over each one and asked the Holy Spirit to fill the now-empty places with His presence.

One painful memory caused physical reaction: shortness of breath and pains in my chest. As I prayed about other memories, the pain increased, then left me in what seemed to be three waves. I was then overcome by the greatest peace. I thought I was floating, yet I knew I was sitting. Immediately another memory came and I saw a connection in my life I had never seen before, between the previous memory and the one that followed.... I found myself getting free from the burden of this stronghold.

Until that time of special prayer, I had not seen the root of my problem. The memory had to do with my fourteenth birthday when my mother decorated my room with pornography. Holidays with my mother were always hard. They were usually non-events. At best I was neglected, at worst I was wounded in some way. For example, when I was twelve she promised to take me to the circus as my Christmas present that year. She took me to see *The Exorcist* instead, because that's what she wanted to do. I remember my mother forcing our way past the line of good church folk who were protesting the vile subject matter of that film. One woman even confronted her. She said to my mother, "You ought to be ashamed of yourself for taking your young child to see that evil movie." My mother didn't care. Later in the theater, when I complained I was scared, she knocked the snot out of me and made me sit in the concession area by myself until it was over. She was insufferable the rest of the day. She was mad because I "ruined her day."

In my first book, *Worst of Mothers...Best of Moms*, I told the story of my thirteenth birthday and the beating I received from her because I had threatened to run away. However, on my fourteenth, my mother was unusually attentive and affectionate. She planned a party with cake and ice cream—the only time that ever happened. For many of you reading this, it will be difficult to comprehend, but putting graphic posters of naked women all over my bedroom walls and ceiling was the nicest thing my mother ever did for me. It was misguided for sure, but for her it was at least some attempt to connect.

The deed alone would challenge any emotionally healthy child not to grow up with some inclination for more of that harmful excrement. For an emotionally starved kid like me, it was a behavioral attachment and badly needed love expressed in an unhealthy and unproductive way. As I journeyed through my adolescence, anytime I felt alone, rejected, or unloved (which was often), I would gaze upon those gifts of love from my mother (or other images like them) and find temporary physical pleasure to mask my inner emotional pain. Certainly, a lot of that was caused by my raging teenage hormones, but it was exacerbated by deeper human need.

That wasn't the first time I went through that kind of "deliverance session." Mama Joyce had led me through a similar time of prayer the first summer I worked at the camp she and her husband Daymond operated. I learned a great deal from her over the years about the power of spiritual warfare to take down the mental and emotional citadels that keep individuals captive to their problems.

Healing is a lot like peeling back the multiple layers of a stinky onion. It's not a one-and-done proposition. It's a process more than an event. The top layers are fairly easy to remove, but as you get closer to the center, the more onerous it is to do without shedding some tears. Now imagine peeling away those many layers required distinct methods of removal for each one. I believe personal healing is like that. Although He could, God doesn't do it just once, and He rarely does it the same way twice. At least He hasn't with me. Consider how many different methods Jesus used to heal the blind in the gospels. Depending on how you count them, there are three or four. Sometimes he touched those He healed. Sometimes He just spoke and declared their healing. Sometimes He required action, such as washing in the river, and yet other times nothing was required at all. Sometimes those who received healing initiated the interaction with Jesus and other times it was Jesus who acted on His own initiative.

I think what we are supposed to learn from these various accounts is that the manner of healing is not the central focus. It's not the method, it is the man—Jesus—who works. We humans often get caught up in doing things a certain way because it worked once, and we lose sight of the one who does the real work. We must be careful we don't get stuck on the method, or the mode, and miss the mission He is doing in our lives.

The upper levels of our injury may be removed by common means, with human intervention. There's nothing wrong with those things. The deepest levels, I believe, require something more than natural man has to offer. Those inner skins require the supernatural. When the disciples failed to free the helpless child possessed by a demon, Jesus told them, "This kind only comes out by prayer and fasting."

It had been two years since a friend of mine left an abusive relationship. She allowed the necessary time to heal before dating again. But all it took was an attempted romantic hug from a new friend to reopen the pain inflicted earlier. Why?

It's frequently said that, "Time heals all wounds." or "Give it time and it will be fine." That is deceitfully untrue. Some have given a lifetime for their wounds to scab over and heal, but it just hasn't happened. Instead of genuine healing, time has only brought disfigurement and deeper hurt. The bleeding has stopped, so to speak, but the pain is still very present, living just beneath the surface.

Healing does often take time, but time never heals anything. It can't. Time has no healing properties of itself. The scars that are formed over time just mask the wounds. Only God heals. He heals by surgery (restoration) of the heart. He heals by therapy (renewing) of the mind. He heals with the salve of love and balm of truth. It is never, though, a passive process. It doesn't just happen on its own. The Lord will prompt. He will prod. He will motivate using any means at His disposal, and He has a lot of means at his disposal. Yet we who are injured must ask. We who are hurt must seek. We who are in pain must knock. And we who are broken will be made new. That's a promise. God wants it more than we do, and He will hound us till we get it. That's what grace does.

The Lord has been good to me in so many ways. He has set me free from my haunting past. He has taken all the horrible things of my childhood and recycled them into a useful life. Nothing, including my pain, has been wasted with God. He has repurposed my problems for His purposes. All the filthy garbage of my past has been recycled into something beautiful, and has ultimately worked for the good. I know without a doubt He can do that for you as well. The process will not be the same as mine. Some of it might be similar, but most of it won't. Each person's story of harm is unique. It stands to reason, then, each person's story of healing will be too. The only thing in common is the God of Grace.

Bottom Line: All injury in this world comes at the hands of the created. From the heart of the creator flow all the cures.

3
Confronted

I feared there would be a dead child on my caseload,
all because I did not properly do my job.

ALL CHILDREN COME INTO THIS WORLD the same — completely helpless. They are utterly weak and powerless. Their size, age, and immaturity (lack of knowledge and experience) naturally make them easy targets for every social ill and human evil.

I became keenly aware of this harsh reality when I worked in Anchorage, Alaska, as a child abuse investigator. Of course, I already knew abuse on a personal level, growing up victimized myself. After seven years of undergraduate and graduate school, I also understood it academically. In the 10–40 degrees below zero winter of 1989, I witnessed this truth in a rather cold, profound way.

Early one morning I came to work at the Division of Family and Youth Services (DFYS) where I had been employed for nearly two years in the Intake Unit. It was my full-time job to investigate Reports of Harm (ROH) to children. Most days I investigated three to six such reports and would, on any given day, "substantiate" one to three of them. Substantiated cases resulted in either a number of services being forced upon the offending guardians as a way of mitigating concerns for the ongoing welfare of the children, or physically removing the young victims from their homes and placing them into protective custody until a Family Court Judge could determine whether or not the State had probable cause to take such drastic action. If I did my job right, the court could do its job. From there, someone else took over the case and it was no longer my concern.

On average, I removed at least one child from his or her family every day I went to work. That was never an easy task, even when it was so blatantly evident it needed to happen. There were many times I worked late into the evening, calling the list of foster homes, desperately searching for someone willing to take the children bouncing off the walls of my drab government office. Sometimes, when I dropped those little ones off at a state-approved foster home, I left wondering if I had just done more harm than good.

The entire process takes a huge emotional toll on anyone who performs it. High employee turnover is a natural result and, of course, that tends to overwhelm the system. In less than two years, I'd gained second in seniority in my unit. I was 27.

The extent of my training at DFYS consisted of spending the first day reading the thick Operations Manual. The second day I was handed my first case. It was sink or swim. It wasn't a simple or clear-cut case either. The child had clearly been hit. There were welts from a belt on his legs. He said he got "whipped" by his mom. But was it child abuse? I wasn't sure. I'd been given a lot worse by my mother for lesser reasons and didn't think much about it at the time, or since. I thought every kid got punished that way at home and at school. Not only had I been spanked by the principal at nearly every school I attended in the south, I sometimes got it from the teachers too. My fifth grade spelling teacher gave her students a stiff whack on the backside with a paddle she kept on her desk for every word missed on the weekly test. She called them "motivation taps." Since I was a horrible speller my butt would be pretty red and sore when I left her room every Friday, but I was more embarrassed than hurt. Since it was so common, I never questioned it.

My social work education and the child protection statutes contradicted my thinking on this issue. Conferring with my supervisor, who had no such hesitation, set me straight. Her clarity confronted my long-held notions about my upbringing. After that day I started seeing what happened to me for what it was — child abuse. I ended up taking custody of the child from his elementary school where I had interviewed him alone and without his parent's knowledge.

Back then the philosophy was, "when in doubt, protect." Since I couldn't remember every part of the procedure I'd read the day before, I took him back to my office and notified the parents by phone I had their child, and said they needed to be at Family Court the next morning. They had to take my word he was safe and would be all right. Can you imagine being the parent on the other end of the line? Worst yet, can you imagine being the child picked up by a stranger and left with people he didn't know, in a place that was unfamiliar.

Because of my "vast" experience, and because we were always short staffed, I was assigned a lot of the high priority and difficult cases that winter. It would be my last winter doing that stressful job.

That particular dreary morning the sun didn't rise until after 10:00 AM, and then it was just kind of dusky until the sun set around 3:00 PM. In other words, it was a typical January day in the Great White North. I was already scheduled to be in court on a case of three small siblings I had removed the day before from a "crack house" where I had found them in deplorable conditions, barely clothed, sick, and obviously malnourished. I was in and out before most of the strung-out adults knew I was even there. Physical exams would later reveal they had suffered significant maltreatment in their short lives. Of all the cases assigned to me during my tenure, I was the proudest of my work that day. It was the reason I showed up every morning. It was the "why" behind the "what."

The following day would be my worst.

Waiting on my desk was a red folder with a Priority One ROH. (The sight of a red folder, despite its content, still causes me a little anxiety.) That meant the department had twelve hours to investigate the report, and the clock was already ticking since we had received it in the middle of the night. An emergency room physician had disclosed suspicious injuries to an infant child. I immediately called the hospital, but when I couldn't speak to the doctor, I asked to speak with the social worker on duty who actually made the report. She communicated to me she had personally spoken with the child's parent and her paramour and informed them of the mandatory report to our office. They seemed cooperative and, in her opinion, gave a reasonable explanation for the child's injury. It seemed to be all just routine to her, as if she was checking off something she was required to do.

She went on to tell me the family was waiting to go home, but the hospital wouldn't release the patient until someone from DFYS (me) gave the okay. Since the social worker seemed fine with discharging them, I granted the needed permission, and I asked her to inform them I would do a home visit later in the day after my court appointment.

As I was heading out the door to go to court, I received a call from the physician. He was furious. In loud, animated tones he said, "I can't believe you are so stupid and careless to release a helpless infant who could very well die at the hands those crazy, lying parents." Needless to say, I asked for further explanation of the injuries and what he thought was the cause.

According to the irate doctor, the baby had an unusual hairline skull fracture. The parents claimed the baby rolled out of bed in the middle of the night and hit his head on the floor. I inquired how high the child would have to fall to sustain such an injury as he described. He said at least ten to twelve feet onto a solid surface, like concrete. Oh no! I knew I had messed up badly.

I quickly found my supervisor, told her what had just taken place, and asked her to cover my court case. I left immediately in the desperate hope of catching them as they arrived home. In my rush, I did not follow certain procedures that I would normally have done before visiting a questionable address.

I nervously arrived at the home not long after the family did. They greeted me and were pleasant and cooperative. I asked the usual set of questions, made the customary notes, and got a good look at the baby. There were no visible injuries. I would not have known anything was wrong if I'd not spoken earlier to the doctor.

Then I asked the mother to show me where the child slept and where he fell. Both ushered me to the child's bedroom and pointed to a single mattress lying on a carpeted floor. They explained they woke up to him crying and found him on the floor. After they couldn't get him to stop crying, they took him to the hospital as a precaution.

I asked a few more questions for clarity and to stall long enough for me to sort out in my head the next move. They repeated the story almost verbatim, as if rehearsed. He did more of the talking than she did. I paused, calmly reached into my case, pulled out a document and handed it to them as I said, as I had said so many times before that day, "By the power vested in me by the State of Alaska, I am taking this child into protective custody. Please hand me the baby."

Despite the fact children come into this world helpless and vulnerable, the Creator, in His wisdom, designed it so they would be raised by two loving parents: one of each sex so the child would learn from, and be better able to relate to, both. With little effort, these two adults are emotionally bonded to their offspring and will unselfishly and even sacrificially protect and serve their every need. But what if it doesn't happen?

The natural order provides additional support by an extended family. All kinds of resources, including the knowledge that only comes from experience, are there for the young parents and especially the children. Two sets of grandparents, aunts, uncles, cousins, and even siblings can serve as a critical second layer of protection and care. But what if that doesn't happen?

God would then have a faith community fill the need. It not only contributes religious instruction and moral support to the family, it also steps in during times of real need with extra resources and assistance. The Church serves as an important third layer of care around those children who are lacking full support from the first two layers. But what happens if there is no community of faith to call upon?

Then the society at large, whose general role is to impart a sense of cultural identity and belonging, fills in the missing pieces, and when needed, forces its authority onto the fractured family system in order to protect and care for the child. What happens when the societal authorities fail to do their job?

That is why I was there that day. I represented the "society at large" for that helpless infant. I was an actor for the State, to perform the duty only the State could do—remove children from their parents if it is deemed "in the best interest of the child." Yet I was doing a poor job of it.

The mother began verbally assaulting me with every kind of offense imaginable. The mother's boyfriend began shoving me in the chest, causing me to step backwards out of the room and toward the front door. Trying to maintain my composure, I kept repeating it was necessary for me to take the baby with me. When we got to the front door, he slapped the side of my head, grabbed my shirt, and shoved me out of the house. He then slammed and locked the door.

Those were the days before cell phones, so I quickly got into my car and drove to the nearest gas station to use a public pay-phone. I called my supervisor, who told me to hang tight and wait for the police. In pretty short order, two cars and four officers arrived. I told them how appreciative I was for their quick and heavy response. They chuckled as they asked if I knew with whom I was dealing. That was the thing I had failed to do when I left my office—a criminal background check.

They informed me that the mom's boyfriend was "a very bad player" and there was an active warrant for his arrest for assault and battery. They went on to say he had a long "rap sheet," and they had been looking for the "punk" for several weeks. Awkwardly I laughed and told the officers that I had found him. They didn't share my morbid sense of humor. I followed closely behind them in my car as they went to the house. It was too late, though. Mom, baby, and the violent boyfriend were already gone, and there were no clues as to where they might be.

Back at my office I tried to concentrate on the large pile of Priority Two (48 hours) and Priority Three (72 hours) cases waiting on my desk, but I was too distracted. My anxious mind repeatedly played out every dark scenario. I feared I would have a dead child on my caseload, all because I did not properly do my job. Yes, I was concerned for the well being of the child, but I also knew how his death could ruin my career and my life. Too distraught to drive the snowy roads home on my own, Karen picked me up after work. I burst out crying, like the panicked man I was, the moment I got safely inside the car. When I arrived home, I hugged my own small children longer than usual that night.

I was miserable for the next couple of days, praying hard for God's divine intervention. I went through the motions of doing my job, but I'm afraid I did it with obvious agitation and heightened self-criticism.

Then on the third day, out of the blue, I received a call from an attorney claiming to represent the mother and boyfriend, who he said were with him in his office. He wanted to negotiate the surrender of the child to the State based, of course, on certain conditions. I politely outlined our case and told him there would be no bargaining. I made it as clear as I could the parents had no choice but to turn the infant over to me. He hung up.

The lawyer called again about ten minutes later and tried a different approach, this time with a lot fewer conditions on the table.

Again, I reminded him of the State's position, and with a harsher tone, demanded they turn the baby over to DFYS immediately. He hung up a second time.

I thought he would call again. In fact, I was counting on it. This time I had an idea. I looked up the address of the attorney and asked my supervisor to answer my phone if he called again and to do everything possible to keep him on the line as long as she could. Then I called the police and asked them to meet me at the lawyer's office where they would find their fugitives.

Four officers burst into the attorney's office, and despite his boisterous protest, arrested the boyfriend on the spot. I followed right on their heels but was grievously disappointed to see the baby was not in the room. Then something amazing happened — something that so clearly illustrated the power of an abuser over his victims. As soon as the handcuffs were securely on the boyfriend, and the mother was surrounded by the safety of law enforcers, she began confessing everything. Her attorney insisted she stop, but I think he saw the whole thing was useless and didn't try much after that. Two officers remained behind while I interviewed the mother in the attorney's office. She explained how it all happened.

The night of the report, the baby had been crying for hours, as babies will sometimes do. The mother tried everything she knew to calm and quiet him. Her boyfriend grew more and more aggravated and began demanding the child stop. At first he started hitting her (something he apparently did often). At some point he finally had enough, picked the child up by his heels, and slammed him against the bedroom wall. He stopped crying. After the unconscious infant didn't respond, they took him to the hospital and, in a rush, made up the poorly conceived tale.

I would learn later there was a great deal more to the story. The mother was a topless waitress at The Great Alaska Bush Company, a popular Anchorage strip club, and her boyfriend was really her pimp, who was "helping" her earn extra money on the side. When the mother got pregnant, he encouraged her not to abort as she first planned but to deliver the child so she could nurse it. A nursing woman has enlarged breasts, which brings in more cash in the shady business of selling sex. It's much cheaper than getting breast implants, which she planned to do with the extra money she made on the side.

For some reason, probably only a therapist could understand, learning the rest of the story took more of a psychological toll on me than anything else that happened in that, or any other, case. I could relate to a woman failing to protect her child because of the threat of violence. I could understand how a person, particularly one not bonded to a child, could snap in a fit of rage and hurt a crying baby. Shaken Baby Syndrome occurs even at the hands of decent people who, in a moment of mental and emotional detachment from the consequences of their actions, do something they would never do in a right state of mind. To be completely honest, I was dangerously close to committing this life-threatening act the night I pleaded with God to help me raise my newborn son. Nevertheless, I could not fathom any mother's willful exploitation of the child she birthed for her own wicked selfishness.

It was not maltreatment forced by deep poverty. It was not drug-induced neglect. Mental illness was not a factor in the abuse of this innocent child. Sickness, desperation, or chaos had nothing to do with it. All the usual suspects were absent. The basis for this crime against nature was a calculated, self-centered choice. It was mistreatment of a precious child for the love of money. That cut me to the core. It impacted me more than any of the horrible abuse and neglect cases I had witnessed the previous eighteen months. Perhaps it stirred memories and emotions associated with my own abusive past and of my whoring mother who so freely, and so frequently, abandoned me for the sake of another no-good man and her own destitute lifestyle.

#20. Parents or Community

Do children belong to their parents or to their communities? Are children citizens of a society or private members of families? How we respond is critically important. If we say that children are first and foremost citizens of society, then the rights of parents are threatened as they lose authority to raise their children as they see fit.

However, if we say that children are only members of families, then communities have no authority or responsibility for their well-being. Both are true at the same time. It starts with parents, but it ends with society. Families are the primary unit of society; their rights must be guarded and their autonomy always protected.

However, the more we see the child as a part of a community, not just the family, the more likely we will regard conceiving and raising that child as tantamount to entering a contract with the community. And, it is that "social contract" that protects the child and holds parents responsible for their privileged role.

StraightTalkwithRobertDay.com

Paternity could not be established, and there were no extended family members who qualified or cared enough to take the baby. The mother eventually gave up her parental rights and the child was placed for adoption. The God-created order for protection, care, and blessing for that little one simply did not exist at any level I outlined above: no immediate family, no extended family, no church family. It never existed. The only hope the child had rested in the authority and power of the state alone. To our credit, we have built a system in the United States to address that need. Sadly, it has many inherent flaws, is usually overwhelmed, and even more problematic, can easily fall prey to political misuse.

However, I'm going to let you in on a secret. I'm going to tell you the real cause of the system's problems — the state is a terrible parent. It's not that the system is doing a bad job and if we could only fix it everything would be fine. No, the system is doing the wrong job. The state can only act after the damage has been done, after a crime has been committed, after irrevocable harm has been inflicted.

We must meet the needs of these vulnerable children and distressed families early. We are obligated to start our interventions when the first signs of trouble appear. The best family for any child is their own family. The best home for any child is their own home. If we wait for a child to be abused, they lose both their family and their home, at least temporarily. In truth, they may never get it back, even if they are returned. In child welfare, an ounce of prevention truly is worth a pound of cure.

That is why I like Safe Families for Children. Started in Chicago, this program is a volunteer-driven, professionally supported, Christian alternative to the foster care system. It really is more of a movement than a program. At the time of this writing, Safe Families for Children is offered in nearly 30 states, and all without federal funding or oversight. Patrick Henry Family Services is an implementing agency for the program in Virginia. We are excited about the impact it is already having for vulnerable children and distressed families. We are equally thrilled by the renewed spirit it is bringing to the cooperating churches.

What caused me to finally give up and leave the state's work of rescuing the most defenseless in our society? It certainly wasn't the suffering children. It wasn't even their horrible caregivers, and trust me, I saw some pretty bad stuff. One of the last cases I took to court involved the sexual abuse of an eight-month-old baby girl by her father, as an act of revenge on his wife for not giving him sex when he wanted it. I was there when the doctor examined the child. With a magnifying glass, he showed me the vaginal evidence that the baby had been sexually abused. What little energy I had left for my job was used up on that one. Yet, that kind of behavior from parents isn't what ultimately discouraged me.

In the end, it was my disillusion with the system that prompted resignation. Finally, I just got fed up with the impersonal, idiotic, bureaucratic maze that often swallowed up children and destroyed fragile families all in the name of doing what was in "the best interest of children."

Here's an inconvenient truth: some of the institutions charged with the care and protection of our future are little more than warehouses of lost childhoods. There are many fine people working in the system who are doing it for all the right reasons. There are also many who are not. Nevertheless, the system has a life of its own, and is bigger than the good or bad people who are on the front lines everyday.

I would end up back in the system several years later. Although this time I was at the other end of it. In 2003, Karen and I were very busy raising our four children. Our two oldest were in high school, and our youngest was about to turn eight. Life was full and busy, and we were blessed. Nonetheless, we also felt something was missing. We had often talked over the years about fostering, and maybe adopting. I had started my career as a child abuse investigator. I'd seen the need firsthand. So after much thought and prayer (which included our children) we decided to become foster parents.

I still remember taking the mandatory classes and wondering what we were getting ourselves into. The instructor was careful to warn all the prospective foster families they would not be getting babies but instead would most likely be getting teenagers (which we had put on our application we didn't want).

In our three years as foster parents we were blessed with both. We cared for a precious baby directly from the Neonatal Intensive Care Unit of the hospital. He was our first placement. We agreed to foster him with the likelihood we would adopt. For one full year we loved Richie as our own. He cried for nearly six months, trying to get clean from the drugs in his system. It took all of us taking turns, caring for him 24/7. Yet we were prepared to make him a permanent member of the family. Then on the day after his first birthday, just as he was finally healthy and happy, he was returned to his parents. It was the hardest day of foster parenting we had, but we would gladly do it again.

We also cared for a young teen girl from a very poor family for nearly two years before she was finally reunited with them. I won't lie. There were some difficult days with Michelle, but we got through them. We gave her opportunities she never had at her house. Just like our other kids, she took swimming and dance lessons and played basketball. She went with us on a family trip to Alaska, during which the boundaries of her world greatly expanded. We watched her grow and heal, to some degree, in her time with us. Despite the advantages we could give her (the safety of our home, the security of routine, and the peace of a Christian environment) she always longed to return home. The state, though, couldn't seem to decide what it was going to do. Finally, after her third case manager quit, we decided to advocate on her behalf and convinced the judge it was time for her to be reunited with her family.

Often we were tempted to think she would be better off staying with us. Certainly she would have advantages her poverty-stricken family would never be able to give her. Without a doubt, we could provide her with nicer things. Even more significantly, she would experience far less drama and dysfunction if she remained with us. Nonetheless, we became convinced that we were helpless to fix the deep grieving of not being with the family of her birth, the painful feelings of doubt and rejection she consistently struggled with, and the inescapable crisis of identity that would continue to play out in multiple negative ways. We testified at family court it was time for Michele to return home. The judge agreed.

The best home for any child is their own. The best family for any child is their own. Sometimes that's just not possible. That is certainly a great tragedy, perhaps even the greatest of all tragedies.

Regardless, before we rip them from their roots, we better make sure we aren't forcing our middle-class values on these poor families as the standard of what is in their best interest. We inflict a world of hurt on kids when we take them from their families, even if it is justified and temporary. There is no escaping that fact.

It's never an easy call. There are no crystal balls, slide rules, or computer programs that can tell us what the outcome will be. It's paramount, then, we must make those decisions with the utmost care, forethought, and purpose. The success of children and the integrity of families is at stake.

The reason we work so hard for reunification in the ministries and programs of Patrick Henry Family Services is because that's what the children want. It also just so happens to also be what children need. It's certainly what they deserve. Sadly, it doesn't always get to happen. When it doesn't, we have a long and arduous task of helping those children heal and grow.

Claudia Fletcher, our Chief Program Officer at Patrick Henry Family Services and mother of twelve adopted children, helped me to understand just how easily we could meet the need of every foster child if only the church was thoroughly engaged.

The United States has nearly 115,000 orphaned kids in the foster care system waiting to be adopted. Some wonder how this is possible in a country with 60 million Christian families. Surely, there are 115,000 missional families in America, right? Missional families, for example, embrace the redemptive mission of God and practice "true religion" in their local communities. Remember James 1:27?

Obviously there are Christian families who adopt. I know several. And there are many great adoptive parents who are not Christians, and that's good. But we have to ask the question. Why can't 60 million families provide loving homes for 115,000 kids? In Virginia, where our ministry is located, there are more churches than there are children in foster care. Certainly each church could manage to take one child under its care.

Missional Christians in America, those who practice biblical hospitality and are concerned with fulfilling the Great Commission, could eliminate the foster care system tomorrow. So why haven't we? The American Dream. We would first have to stop chasing after the American Dream of comfort and ease long enough to fulfill an orphan's dream of having a permanent family, and that's neither easy nor is it comfortable.

There is hardly a day goes by that I don't think of those two precious children who were once a part of our family. I'm so glad we opened our home and our hearts to them. They made each of us better people and our family unit stronger. Parenting my kids made me a better person. Parenting other people's children not only made me a better person, it also made me a more authentic child of God.

I don't know how many times I've heard someone say they could never be a foster parent because it would be too painful to send them back. My response is twofold. First of all, that's exactly the kind of people who should take these children into their homes, where they will be loved and wanted. Secondly, they need to get over it because it's not about them. It's about the kids. Not caring for a hurting child because you might get hurt yourself is about the most self-centered thing I've ever heard. Forgive me, but it is.

Bottom Line: We can't rescue vulnerable children without also restoring their families. Until that's possible, the very best way to help them is to bring them into our own homes and make them part of our own families.

4
Broken

*There was nothing to do, but do what I had sung a hundred times
as a parishioner and pastor—I surrendered all.*

S OMEWHERE I HEARD, most likely in a sermon, "God can't really use a man until he's broken." Maybe because the message was meant for me, I've never forgotten it. Of course, the preacher didn't mean to suggest God is limited in any way by anybody. He did intend to convey that a person's ego can get in his own way.

One of the many things I've always appreciated about the Bible is that it doesn't hold back any punches. It tells the entire magnificent story, mess and all. The ugly weakness of every character throughout Scripture, even the heroes, is laid open and bare for all to see. They are all flawed. Many of them deeply. It's as if the author of the Book of Books is trying to make a point about the nature and power of sin and the desperate need for a redeemer.

Let's now peel back another layer, a really deep one, that revealed a huge fault in me and caused a particular type of pain for a good part of my adult life. First, some context.

For some time now, I've had a love-hate relationship with the local church. During my childhood and adolescence, the local church was a safe and nurturing place. There were so many different kinds of churches, in so many places, that were the Body of Christ incarnate to me. The denomination didn't matter. I didn't know the difference, and probably wouldn't have cared if I did. The size was inconsequential. I was not impressed. Doctrine wasn't an issue. I didn't need that, nor would I have understood it. I sought refuge in the local church because it was not like my family. I went there to escape my disorderly world. I got up, and got myself to the nearest church whenever I could because I felt accepted and even loved. Like moths to a light in the darkness of night, I was drawn to church.

To be completely honest, though, I don't feel that way anymore. The affection I once held for the local church has waned over the years. Let's just say, I'm no longer attracted to it as I once was. The oasis has disappointedly turned out to be a mirage. Yet my desire to be a part of what I believed, and knew to be true, about the church as a child is still very much alive. So what changed?

My feelings for the church began to turn when I became a minister and started working in the church. I have served seven churches spanning a little over twenty years in three states:

Calvary Baptist, Corbin KY—part-time Youth Minister.
Baptist Tabernacle, Louisville KY—part-time Church Social Worker
First Baptist, Anchorage AK—part-time Youth Minister, then full-time Associate Pastor
First Baptist, Ketchikan AK—full-time Pastor
Alliance Bible, Anchorage AK—full-time Senior Pastor
Newcomb Baptist, Newcomb TN—full-time Pastor
Word of Life, Williamsburg KY—bi-vocational Pastor

Like the seven churches in John's Revelation, each had reasons for God to both commend and condemn them. My presence in them simply added to both sides of the ledger.

When I turned eighteen and had to register for Selective Service, the gentleman at the post office asked if I was a Baptist. It wasn't on the forms so I replied, "Yes, does it matter?"

He answered, "In the event of a war, they'll call up all you Baptists first."

"Really? Why is that?"

"Cause everybody knows Baptists make the best fighters."

He chuckled. I politely smiled. After serving on staff of five Baptist churches, I know exactly what he meant. Sadly, though, it's not funny. And, by the way, that distinction is not just reserved for the Baptists. When I served in the church in a part-time capacity, I only partly saw the problem. Once I served the church full-time, I saw the problem fully. I got a good glimpse behind the curtain only to discover there was a lot of smoke and mirrors.

While I don't pastor today, my role at Patrick Henry Family Services puts me in a number of churches every year. I have the privilege of presenting the ministry and sometimes preaching the message. In my personal and professional lifetime, I've been in hundreds of churches all across the theological spectrum and in many places across this country. From my perspective, the local church seems to have lost sight of its mission. Somehow over time, congregations started serving a particular model of *doing* church, and drifted away from the unique call of *being* the church. I know it sounds kind of boorish to say, but I do think it is the fundamental issue. I firmly believe the single greatest issue in our world today is not hunger or homelessness. It's not child abuse or bad schools. It's not the breakdown of the family, the scourge of drugs, or out-of-wedlock births. It's not even crime or terrorism. While all of those things are horrific problems, none of them are *the* problem. The single greatest need in the world today is for the church to be the church again. If I were granted the power to fix one thing in this broken world, I would use it to correct the mission drift of the Church. Everything else is a symptom of a church off mission. This became abundantly clear to me during my first pastorate.

526. God is God

There was probably no more a faithful servant to God than the prophet Ezekiel. He did whatever the Lord required, without question or hesitation. Of all the characters in Scripture, Ezekiel is the only one God refers to as Son of Man, a title Jesus would give himself.

One day God interrupted this remarkable man's life and ministry. The Lord announced to the prophet He would take the life of his wife, and Ezekiel would be forbidden to mourn her loss. In a rare word from the servant of God, he tells us what happened and how he responded. "So I spoke to the people in the morning," Ezekiel says, "and in the evening my wife died. And in the morning I did as I was commanded."

God, being God, has the right to interrupt our lives for His own purposes. When he does, may each of us respond with the same trusting obedience, and may we also be able to say, "I did as I was commanded."

StraightTalkwithRobertDay.org

I was 29 in the summer of 1990 when I was extended a call to be the pastor of First Baptist Church of Ketchikan, Alaska, "where fish and men go up Creek Street to spawn." Armed with a master's degree in Social Work, a few years of part-time youth ministry experience, and an overabundance of confidence, I thought I was more than ready for the sacred task. Some of the congregation, on the other hand, were less than enthusiastic. For the first year or so, some of the members would introduce me to visitors as their "baby preacher." I would sometimes refer to them as "God's Frozen People." Since it was so difficult to get someone to come to that isolated island community and shepherd a flock of misplaced Southern Baptists with a reputation for discord and disunity, they were generally glad to have me. I was, in the beginning at least, more than happy for the opportunity.

Nestled tightly between mountains and the ocean of the Inside Passage, Alaska's fourth largest city is a uniquely beautiful place. Everyone should visit, but please don't act like typical tourists by asking silly questions. Yes, Alaska is bigger than Hawaii. No, it's not next to it. Yes, the businesses take American money. No, it's not all right to stop in the middle of the road to take pictures. It's definitely worth the trip, but bring rain gear. With an average of 228 inches of precipitation a year, sunshine can be a rare treat. Moss even grows on the inside of vehicles. It makes Seattle look like an Arizona desert.

The Pastorium (as the church called it) had a wonderful view of the inlet. From our living room we could watch the big cruise ships, fishing boats, floatplanes, and the airport ferry, all masterfully navigating the narrow channel without incident. We saw dozens of Bald Eagles every day, and occasionally would be treated to a pod of Orca passing through.

For a young family like ours cutting our teeth in the ministry, despite its beauty, Ketchikan was a spiritually dark place. It quickly became obvious I was in way over my head, and in less than six months I was looking for a way out. All my hopes and youthful dreams about leading a church were destroyed. Remember what happens to the moth and the light?

I simply couldn't fathom, for example, how a group of mature adults could argue for nearly an hour over buying a new vacuum cleaner versus repairing the existing one. They eventually agreed to take a vote on a motion to have someone's cousin take a look at it before they would decide between the two options. We went without a vacuum at the church for nearly three months because no one wanted to offend the member with the lazy cousin who wasn't "getting around to it." I was clearly operating beyond my abilities to lead people who were more than twice my age but did the work of God with less than half their heart. At least, that was my perspective at the time.

I struggled to lead the congregation. I was even more dismayed by the considerable needs in the community. I simply didn't have the pastoral skills, or spiritual strength, to deal with so many wounded people who had so many deep needs: substance abuse, depression, sexual transgressions, and mental illness. My Social Work skills sometimes proved helpful, but for the most part were ineffective within the context of the church. I needed tools for what was essentially a spiritual battle.

We once had a visitor bring a handgun to the morning service with a credible plan to kill herself right there among us, and she would have succeeded if her odd behavior had not gotten my attention. She caught my eye just before I went to the podium to start the service. In her hand was a brown paper bag, and she seemed very anxious. I went to the back to greet her and to see if she was all right. She handed me the bag and asked if I would hide it from her.

"What's in it?"

"A gun."

"Why did you bring a gun with you to church?"

"To kill myself."

I called a deacon over, handed him the bag, and told him to lock it in my office. Then I asked another deacon to sit next to her. With my encouragement, she sat down and stayed for the service. When it was over, we went to my office and she told me everything that led up to that morning and the grizzly plan she had hatched. She said my kindness in greeting her caught her off guard. The same woman later became a dear family friend who stayed at our house and watched our children on many occasions.

Once, I was asked to provide counseling for a young couple who had been married for just two weeks. They were having troubles and were already thinking of divorce. I asked them how long they had been together before they were married. "Two weeks" was their answer. Despite my best effort, they remained married for only two more weeks before filing for divorce: his third, her fourth.

There was an active youth group that was led by a volunteer, a young mom who had a good rapport with teens and seemed very capable of doing more. So I hired her full-time as soon as I had the chance. She was the daughter of one of the leading families in the church, and her husband was an active member. It seemed everything was going great. The group was growing and became involved in several service projects. Then we were hit by a bombshell. The first employee I ever hired and supervised got pregnant by one of the young men in her group who, by the way, happened to be the leader of the Abstinence Club at the high school. Somehow I got stuck with all the blame for that.

My despair increased with each passing month. I felt trapped on that island, which had only twelve miles of road from one end to the other. I needed out of that place, or I needed some kind of help to stay. It was when I tried to leave that I found the support, and the strength, to stay.

A congregation from my home state of Tennessee was interested in having me serve as their pastor. I made a trip to the lower 48 to preach "in view of a call." I told my Ketchikan congregation I would be attending a conference in Las Vegas on evangelism for a week, which was true. I swear. I just didn't tell them the rest of my plans, which included a side trip to the Volunteer State before I returned.

The Tennessee church seemed like the perfect fit. We were culturally in sync. We enjoyed the same foods and spoke the same language (both dialect and meaning). I nailed the trial sermon. (It's not bragging if it's true). Plus, they were offering more money than I was getting in Alaska, which had a much higher cost of living.

Side note: Why does it always seem to be God's will for pastors to move to bigger churches with larger salaries? Seems like He would send some of them to smaller churches. Right? One day I asked the same question to a group of seminary students who were bragging about the size of the churches they were going to after graduation. All had been serving small flocks while at school but were excited about trading in their newly conferred degree for larger churches. A little aggravated by the question, they looked at me a little tongue-tied. Then one of the honest ones said, "God is everywhere. So I follow the money." That statement told me everything I needed to know about how the Church got into its current condition. John Maxwell believes everything rises and falls on leadership, and I believe that is largely the issue.

At the time I was in Ketchikan, I probably had a similar mindset. However, in this case, I wanted to go to Tennessee to flee where I was, not to earn a bigger paycheck. That's still not a good reason. But it looked to me like the will of God in every way.

A small miracle that weekend even seemed to confirm my belief. On the last day of my trip, while going through the lobby of the hotel where I was staying, I purchased two postcards to send back home to my children, but I neglected to buy two postcard stamps to put on them. I just didn't think about it.

Back in my room, I kneeled next to my bed and began to pray. "Lord, if it is your will for me to come to Tennessee, I am ready to come." Then in a rare moment of spiritual maturity, I added, "But, if it is your will for me to remain in Alaska, you better make that abundantly clear because I don't want to stay."

A small voice spoke to my spirit, "Look under the bed."

"Sorry, Lord, I got distracted. If you want me to stay in Ketchikan, please make it clear to me."

"Look under the bed."

"Forgive me, Father, I'm having a hard time concentrating."

"Look under the bed."

"Not sure if I'm hearing you right."

"LOOK UNDER THE BED."

Was I losing my mind? I didn't hear an audible voice that day, but it was as clear as one. I could not go any further until I took a peek under that bed. I turned my head and laid it nearly flat to the floor and looked. I squinted in order to focus on two tiny objects about middle way under the bed. I extended my reach, grasping without clearly seeing, until I finally had them in my hands: two postcard stamps. Not one less than I needed. Not one more than I needed. Exactly what I needed. Amazing! I didn't put them there. I was in that room all week. Room Service had cleaned every day. Yet, they were just the right number of stamps I needed, with just the right amount of postage on them, just when I needed them. And I hadn't even asked the Lord for them.

"If I can take care of a need this small and insignificant," the Lord seemed to say to me, "I can take care of your big needs."

"Yes sir. Thank you, Father. Forgive me, Lord."

I then spent some time in praise and worship and in awe of the God I serve. I took those two 19-cent stamps as a sign I was going to Tennessee. The long flight back to Alaska was peaceful as I dreamed about the future. I was also quickly getting very sick. By the time I arrived home, I felt horrible and was having difficulty breathing. Within 24 hours I was in the emergency room where I was diagnosed with double pneumonia.

For more than a week I was confined to bed, gasping to breathe and trying hard to find a comfortable position to rest. During those miserable few days while I was helpless to do anything, it seemed as if every problem at the church exploded all at once. Already stressed caring for our two toddlers, my very pregnant wife felt the pressure of trying to manage home and church responsibilities. We were both desperately anxious to get the call from Tennessee so we could have something positive to celebrate. Then one day it came, but it wasn't what we were expecting. They didn't want me. I couldn't believe it. After all of that, they picked someone else. I felt hopeless.

Physical discomfort gave way to emotional anguish. Rejection has always been my Achilles Heel. Not so much today, but back then it would lay me out quicker than any virus or bacteria. I did the only thing I could do. In my utter desperation (and lack of distraction from any other demands but to lie in bed), I prayed and cried out to God.

"Lord, you said it was your will for me to be in Tennessee."

"No, you assumed that."

"But Father, I can't stay here."

"Sure you can. You just don't want to."

"No, I can't. I hate it here. I won't stay here."

"Yes, you can. Yes, you will."

After debating with the Lord for a better part of the morning, I finally gave up and made a deal with Him. I'm not sure why I ever think I can strike a bargain with the Sovereign God of the universe.

"All right, Lord, your will be done, but I don't have to like it. If I have to stay, then you are going to have to pastor this church. You are going to have to meet these people's needs and fix their problems, because I sure can't."

Then the Lord said something to me which has forever changed the way I view my ministry. He said it as clearly and as loudly as I have ever heard him say anything to me.

"It's all I have ever wanted. It's all I ever asked of you and the church. I can meet their needs. I can fix their problems. You've made it something else. You've made it about you."

I was a broken man.

There was nothing to do, but do what I had sung a hundred times as a parishioner and pastor—I surrendered all. Please trust me when I say this: there is nothing like the joy of throwing your hands up in the air in sweet surrender and saying, "I give up. I'm done fighting." It was then, at that moment, the Holy Spirit really started my healing process by getting to those cavernous layers of wretched hurt. Although it wasn't as clear then as it is now.

Pride is at the root of our rebellion against God. Our ego is at the center of every sinful deed. The sins committed against me as a child were the result of the pride of others. The sins I committed as an adult were caused by my own arrogance, not the result of abuse and neglect. Did you get that? It's important, so pay attention. The foolish, sinful things I did as an adult were my fault. Mine alone. There may be a childhood reason behind it, but it isn't an excuse to remain angry, or depressed, or impulsive, or combative, or jealous, or bitter, or a thousand other iniquities. Until the pride problem is dealt with properly, every move toward healing will only be hampered and hindered.

The first Sunday after I recovered from pneumonia, I stood before the congregation and recounted the entire story. I didn't hold back anything. I told them I had gone to Tennessee in hopes of leaving. I told them I didn't like living in Ketchikan. I told them I didn't like most of them. At that point I figured I had nothing to lose and everything to gain by being completely honest. If they ran me off, then I would get what I wanted and it wouldn't be my fault. Well, at least that's what I told myself. Rationalization is a sneaky devil. It headquarters in our deceitfully wicked heart with the purpose of making us feel better about our disobedience.

There was a strange silence when I finished. A few heads nodded as if they knew all along. After an awkward pause, I told them something I was certain would get me run out of there on a rail. I announced that, until further notice, I was suspending every program and ministry of the church except Sunday Morning Worship. There would be no Sunday School, Sunday Night or Wednesday Night services, and all committees would be disbanded except the deacon body. I went on to explain the doors of the church would be unlocked and the altar open twenty-four hours a day, every day, for prayer. After forty days of prayer and seeking the Lord, we would see where we were and what we were going to do from that point forward. After reading a prepared statement, I stepped down to the altar, knelt and prayed until the sanctuary was empty. I didn't want to give anybody a chance to argue or debate. I also pleaded with God one more time to let me leave.

To make a long story short, I wasn't fired. Instead, the church got fired up. Revival broke out! It would probably best be described as a Spiritual Awakening. For a little more than two years, the church was energized with new spirit. Nearly every Sunday someone made a significant decision for Christ. People, young and old, were making strong commitments to God. It was during this period I found freedom from pornography that I wrote about earlier. The church grew. The congregation matured. Ministry happened. Individuals were changed. Broken relationships were restored. Deep hurts were healed. We were becoming the glorious body of Christ. As He promised, God was pastoring those people. He was meeting their needs. He was fixing their problems.

My journal entry dated 9.22.92 captured just some of what was happening. "KS told me today that last night she came into the church to pray and AH was there alone [these two women had been bitter towards each other for several years]. KS couldn't get past God telling her to seek forgiveness. She did, and they both wept and prayed together, and for one another. Some people have grown by leaps and bounds so far. ML came by the house yesterday wanting help on getting to a place where she can forgive her uncle of a grave sin. She has changed tremendously. She confessed she had made 're-commitments' in the past that lasted only a few days, but what is happening now in her life seems to be deep and lasting."

I had never seen anything like it before, nor have I seen anything like it since. It was truly awesome, as in the biblical definition of the word. Why?

Forgiveness is a wellness principle. If it's a true movement of the Holy Spirit, the issue of forgiveness will be pressed. As the members of First Baptist Church forgave each other, the church began to experience spiritual health and a communal vitality like it had not seen in decades—maybe ever. There is no healing without first forgiving. I'm sorry if that bothers you, but it's true. There is no escaping that spiritual principle.

One of the longtime members of the church, Barbara Kimball, was especially responsive to the call to prayer. She was one of the most faithful in that regard. She recently released a book on prayer and writes about lessons learned from the 40 days of prayer: *After Midnight Meditations: Seeking God's Light For Myself and Others*. In it she stresses the significance of forgiveness in healing and the role it played in her own spiritual growth.

"For the next several days, one thing after another would be laid on my heart to deal with in the manner God was teaching me. I had confessed all the things I knew had kept a stranglehold on me, but He brought things to my heart and mind I didn't realize were hindering my walk with Him. I forgave those I didn't realize I needed to forgive.... I forgave those I had never been able to forgive or thought I could.... Now I realize my inability to forgive had caused me to fail in my walk as they became stumbling blocks.... He taught me to forgive, and in that forgiveness was peace."

Then as quickly as it had come, it was gone...vanished. It was as if someone had turned off the power to the building. The old familiar darkness quickly returned. It happened one Sunday night at a church business meeting, one of the first we had since that fateful Sunday of transparency, when I tried to get kicked out. Thankfully, the days of debating vacuum cleaners were long gone. This time, though, there was a significant matter before the church regarding a camp they owned and operated. Before the time of revival, it was one aspect of the ministry I enjoyed. We had reached a lot of kids through that camp, and I was pleased to be a part of it. Yet, as the revival grew, the property seemed to become more of a burden than a blessing. It had always been a financial strain on the small congregation, even when we managed to fill the summer with campers. The decision facing the members was whether or not to allow a sister church to take over operations and, thereby, free us to focus on other exciting opportunities. After a great deal of prayer and discussion, a large number of us had come to the conclusion it was the best thing in the long run. Additionally, we believed it would be a blessing to our sister church and, ultimately, to us as well.

The night of the business meeting, however, the sanctuary was filled with some people who had not been to a service of any kind since the revival had broken out. In fact, I had never seen some of the individuals in attendance. That didn't matter, though. In Baptist polity, every member, whether they attend or not, whether they understand the issue or not, whether they are spiritually mature or not, has a vote in the business matters of the church. It's a pure form of democracy, as I was often told by the members. Despite what seemed to be an attempt by someone, or group of someones, to stack the votes in favor of keeping the camp, the motion passed by a tiny margin of precisely three votes.

It was a close call, but the church had managed to make an extremely difficult decision by prayer instead of by politics. Nonetheless, the deacon body, some of whom had not been really participating in the spiritual renewal of the last couple years, decided that three votes was not enough of a majority, and in expressing their fear of a church split over the issue, announced the motion did not pass and would not be voted on again. The decision not only flew in the face of the movement of God, but was also a blatant violation of the church's by-laws. It certainly wasn't "pure" democracy.

Many, including myself, were heartbroken and angry. For us, it wasn't about the camp as much as it was about honoring what we were convinced was the will of God. Looking back I've often wondered if the whole thing was some kind of cosmic test.

For several weeks after that, I tried to go about my work as I had been doing but was frustrated at every turn. The time of renewal had ended. The revival had been snuffed out. The darkness of division and dysfunction had returned. I quickly became discouraged and depressed. Strange things began happening. Someone set our mailbox on fire. Another time, someone threw vomit all over the front seat and dashboard of our minivan. Our kids discovered some kind of idol freshly buried in our backyard. Many folks in the community simply stopped talking to us. I tried harder. I prayed more. Yet nothing changed. This time when I asked the Lord to allow me to leave, I felt I got the go-ahead. Six months later, we were heading back to Anchorage.

Using the 20/20 vision of hindsight, I would do some things differently. A lot of it I wouldn't. I don't think God had me in Ketchikan because He needed me there. No, He had me in that particular place, at that particular time, because I needed to be there to learn a particular lesson. Ketchikan didn't need me. I needed Ketchikan. Interesting enough, of all the churches I pastored, it is the only one I occasionally dream about. In my dreams, I am still there pastoring, or have returned to pastor. It's as if there is some unfinished business there.

God's work in us is always so much bigger than our work for Him. The Lord sent me to America's wettest city to learn and to grow at the Ministry School of Hard Knocks. I'm appreciative of the time spent there, and also thankful for the lives that were changed because I stayed when I wanted so badly to run away.

Bottom Line: God calls us to be faithful, not successful. Those are two entirely different things. From God's viewpoint, living faithfully is the highest form of triumph.

5
Busted

It was hard work being a fake.

THE FIFTH CHURCH I SERVED was a congregation of the faithful belonging to the Christian and Missionary Alliance. I was attracted to the denomination's concept of biblical eldership (which tends to negate some of the problems inherent with congregational rule), their emphasis on sanctification, and their special affection for missions. Those believers knew their Bible and were spiritually more mature than I had seen before in the other churches I served. They also had strong male leadership within their ranks, something I wasn't accustomed to having in the churches I served. For the most part they were a healthy body. I found myself challenged to feed and lead them. I was 34.

In many ways it was good to be back in Anchorage, Alaska's largest city. In fact, half of the state's population lived there. The other half teasingly said the best thing about Anchorage is that it's only ten minutes from Alaska. Sometimes, though, Alaska came to Anchorage. We had moose in our front and back yards, in our driveway, and many times on our street. One summer day, Karen took our children to a neighborhood park. She was sitting on a bench watching them on the playground when a grizzly bear walked between her and the kids. Everyone remained calm and let him pass by.

My growing family and I lived in a lovely, split-level house (the first home we owned), on a street called Bounty. It was a nice neighborhood with lots of kids who often occupied the entire street with their games. It was a wonderful church to serve, and they did a good job of caring for our needs. There were the occasional disputes and challenges, of course, but overall we felt blessed. It was idyllic in almost every way. It was everything I never thought as a child I would ever have or experience.

513. Broken Hopes

Ever since I was a young boy I've enjoyed spending time in the woods. There's a quiet, peaceful aspect of the forest I find refreshing. It's good for my spirit. If we stop to ponder, we can find many life lessons among the trees.

What makes the trees grow? What gives them the nourishment to survive and even thrive? Look at the base of the woodland trees and you will find the answer. It is dead branches and leaves that the tree itself has shed. The things that have died in the tree are what gives it the power to live. Seems like there is something we can learn from that.

Usually, it's the things in our life that have died, the areas of our life where we have suffered loss, the issues that God has pruned, that give us the greatest potential for growth and new life. Trees are fertilized by their own decay, and so we too are improved by trial and refined by broken hopes.

StraightTalkwithRobertDay.org

Then suddenly, it too was gone. This time, however, the responsibility was on me, and me alone. I messed up. Forgetting all the hard lessons learned in Ketchikan, I allowed a little bit of hubris and a whole lot of fear get the best of me.

Alliance Bible Church (ABC) began growing almost immediately after I arrived. Within the year, we were making active plans to relocate to a larger building, and did the second year. Even then we had to start a second service to accommodate the crowd. A Filipino congregation, who had been using the building for their own separate service, decided to merge with us. We had a very diverse congregation that represented four languages and a large number of young families. We were always overflowing with children.

One Sunday I shared my testimony of getting free from pornography and preached about its destructive nature. It was an uncomfortable subject, and telling my role in it was difficult. I thought it would be helpful, yet I was surprised by the magnitude of the response. Over a dozen men came forward during the hymn of response and sought forgiveness for their own involvement in that tasteless trouble. From that day forward, on their own accord, they formed a support group to keep each other accountable. It was a huge blessing to see these men grow in their faith and love for their families.

I enjoyed more normalcy, and greater success, at ABC than I had ever known in my entire broken life up to that time. To be completely transparent, though, it unnerved me.

One of the biggest differences between people living in poverty and those not is the root source of their fear. The middle class tends to fear failure. Their lives center around not failing. The ongoing mantras of the middle class illustrate it: go to college, get a good job, save money, don't go into debt, plan for retirement. It's the opposite for the poor. They tend to fear success. Their lives center around not succeeding. It's not so much in their words as in their actions: drop out of school, quit a good job, don't save money, waste hard-earned income on addictive substances, go deeper in debt. The wealthy, on the other hand, don't seem to be intimidated by either failure or success.

Without realizing it at the time, I grew more and more uncomfortable with the routine of a good life, the responsibility of meaningful work, and most frightful of all, the reckoning God was doing in my heart. While I didn't like it, I understood the many dysfunctions in Ketchikan. It was familiar and somewhat normal to me. In my second pastorate, however, I was the Overseer of people I didn't really understand. For the first time in my life, I was firmly planted in the middle of the middle class. I was living among well-educated people who grew up in solid Christian homes, but it was foreign soil to me. I was living a pretty nice life, but I didn't really know how to, and it was extracting massive amounts of personal energy to pretend I did.

Here is something we must be aware of when working with the poor: just because we can put the poor in a middle-class community, with a middle-class lifestyle, and give them a middle-class job, doesn't mean they become middle class. A person coming out of poverty is typically under-resourced in so many areas of their life, not just financial, that the mental and cultural transition may never fully transpire. Giving people a good paycheck doesn't suddenly compensate for what they may lack in other parts of their life.

There's a family legend that I heard growing up about some of my mother's kinfolk who went up north to find work. They had secured good jobs at a factory in Cincinnati and had checked into a hotel room the night before. They entered the elevator to go to their third-floor rooms. When the door closed behind them, they panicked. They had never been in one before and didn't know how to operate it. The four of them remained in there until someone pushed the bottom to get on. When the doors opened, they quickly fled. They didn't stop until they got all the way back to their home in the mountains of eastern Kentucky the next morning. Their exposure to the unknown and their fear of success had them retreating for their poor, but knowable, lives. They would not be included in the Great Brain Drain out of Appalachia. As far as I know, the four lived and died in the same hollow where they were born.

It's like the summer I coached my son's recreational soccer team. He wanted to play, but the only way he, and a bunch of other kids, were going to get the chance was if I volunteered to lead the team.

I did, even though I had never played soccer. I didn't know the first thing about the rules or strategy of the game. Moreover, the first time I had even seen a game from start to finish was the first time my team played. Nonetheless, every day that summer, I pretended to be a soccer coach. I was the coach by position and title. I wasn't the coach by knowledge or experience. Even more important, I was not the coach because I didn't believe I was a coach. I was woefully unprepared for the role. Putting me in that place, giving me a title, handing me some soccer balls, a rule book, and a schedule didn't suddenly change reality. Not surprisingly, we didn't win a single game. My son and I had a fun time together, which made it well worth the effort.

Every day for four years at ABC, I pretended to be someone, and something, I wasn't. It was largely an act. I had no background or context for being what I was. My children all remember and still tease me about sleeping a lot when they were little. I did. I was fatigued continually from my performance as a Bible scholar, caring shepherd, and confident leader. I was always worn out from the normal drama of family life—from acting like a loving husband, a nurturing father, and a good friend and neighbor. At that time in my life, none of those things came naturally. Very little of it was real. I wanted desperately to be all those things for the people I loved and for the positions I held, but they weren't yet a fully integrated part of me. It was form without substance.

Recently some of us were watching old family videos of when the kids were little. Most of the time the recorder was focused on the children as they played, fought with each other, learned to walk, had birthday parties, or celebrated Christmas. It's the kind of stuff you see in any homemade family film. I was sickened, though, when I saw a couple of glimpses of the real me in those videos. They are brief but stunning. It's obvious I had some serious heart issues at the time. Allow me to say here to my family, especially my wife, I'm deeply sorry. Please forgive me.

It was hard work being a fake. Some of you know exactly what I'm talking about. Even as you read this, you are afraid you'll be discovered. Without judgment, allow me to give you some friendly advice: find help and get real. If you don't, the stress and pressure will eventually cause a crisis. For some, it will be a moral scandal that destroys your ministry. For others of you it will be a mental breakdown, a physical illness, or a failed marriage. There are a hundred and one ways it could happen, but I warn you, it will eventually happen. The truth will catch up to you.

I know you're avoiding counseling because it's going to hurt. You don't want to dig up all that pain you've been suppressing for so long. I totally get that. Think of it this way, though — the pain of therapy is controlled and measured. The pain of self-destruction is not. You can afford the price of counseling. You may not be able to afford the high cost of your life unraveling.

At Alliance Bible I was doing a pretty good job of what my mother would have called "putting on airs." As with my mother, there is something about the hypocrisy of "putting on airs" that offends my cultural sensibilities. A good friend and fellow social worker, Cliff Rosenbohm, used to quote an old southern preacher he knew growing up: "Be who you is. Cause if you is who you ain't, you ain't who you is." That's about as profound as anything I've ever heard. It became a favorite saying at our house. Looking back I can see that insightful quote was a clarion call for me to get real with myself.

There's a theological tension in life. God loves us for who we are, and is simultaneously changing us into someone else — someone better. The work of the Holy Spirit, the Counselor, is to transform us from one degree of glory to the next. No doubt, we must learn to be comfortable in our own skin. We must negotiate a peace treaty with ourselves. At the same time, we must not settle for who we are. We must continually struggle until we are the spitting image of our Savior. At ABC, I got caught up in the unrealistic demands of acting like a Christian instead of just being one. I performed the role of a loving husband and nurturing father, a good pastor, until I could become a "real" one. Eventually, it led to a major identity crisis.

After four years, all that make-believe and fear of success had taken its toll. My emotions were raw and the cistern of courage I drew from daily was finally depleted. The stress of being a pastor, leader, husband, and father was becoming more than I could handle. I could feel myself coming unglued. External pressure was stirring up unresolved childhood pain.

Reading the journal I kept then, I can see the anguish and how I was setting myself up for a conflict. In an entry dated 3.12.97, I wrote: "I realized something last night at the 'Church of Anchorage' meeting. I no longer have a heart for this city—no burden for its people. I'm not sure I have any real affection for my own congregation. I love the Word. I have a burden for teaching its truth. I labor for the benefit of the church, but the people themselves do not stir my heart. O God, why is this? How can this be? Am I so distant from you that I can't feel any of your love for them? Please help me Jesus to have your heart for this congregation and for this city."

Then I wrote something very telling. I began bargaining with God. I started crafting the argument for leaving: "Help me either cry for these people, or take me to a place where I can."

Then I revealed my emotional state: "For I am growing weary of well doing." I also expressed the fear of what I was secretly doing in my deceitfully wicked heart: "I do not want to be a reproach on your name."

By 4.14.97 I was really struggling with it: "God, what are you trying to tell me? The restless nights, lack of joy in the ministry, the critical spirit and apathy tell me something is amiss. Lift me out of this miry clay, for your name's sake."

The entry on 6.17.97 showed I was being tempted with fleeing: "Dear Lord, another Father's Day is approaching and I must find something to preach.... Keep me from wandering away from your will. Help me to learn contentment." Father's Day, and especially Mother's Day, were always the worst. It was never a good time for me to be confronted. That's exactly what happened.

A group of men in the church accosted me one Sunday afternoon about a number of poor decisions I had made (subconsciously I was sabotaging my own success). One by one they went around the conference table expressing their displeasure in the way I was leading the church and their dismay about the direction I was taking it. They were right. They probably could have gone about it differently, but their complaints were valid. I know that today. Looking through the rearview mirror, I believe they were sincerely and lovingly trying to help me. I have since learned there is a big difference between critics and enemies. Our critics are those who are afraid we are wrong and they don't want us to be wrong. Our enemies are those who are afraid we are right and they don't want us to be right. We should honor the first and pray for the second.

I didn't know that then. I just felt betrayed and rejected. You remember what rejection did to me, right? Having little strength remaining, I was overcome by fear and an overdose of pride. Without warning or notice, I resigned from the church the following Sunday. The congregation was shocked, hurt, and disappointed, but I didn't care. No, honestly, I couldn't care. There was nothing left in me to care.

The following three months I was an "emergency hire" at my old place of employment, DFYS. I was enlisted as extra help so they could get their case numbers down in order to maintain their investigative mandate. Once again I was assigned a bunch of the difficult reports. I did quite a few cases involving allegations against foster parents. Those kinds of cases are land mines, with lots of casualties. Sadly, there are some foster parents who abuse their foster, as well as their own, children. Even sadder still, there are many more foster parents being mistreated by the system that recruited and trained them.

The job was meant to be temporary. Even if it wasn't, I wouldn't have stayed long. Eventually my time was over, and I was once again unemployed.

A few weeks later we left Bounty street. We headed back to Kentucky, not knowing where, or how, we would live. The doors had opened on my own proverbial elevator, and like my Appalachian kinfolk decades ago, I fled back to familiar country as quickly as I could. Then I doubled my shame by claiming it was the will of God.

After the fiasco at Alliance Bible Church, I returned to Southern Seminary where I earned a Master of Divinity degree. It seemed like the logical thing to do. I had gotten a social work degree and ended up pastoring churches, for which I seemed poorly equipped. After working hard at three part-time jobs to feed my family, while also carrying a full class load, I received the degree. I was also reconnected with Darrell and Darlene Shirley, the couple who served as youth ministers at my home church when I was a teen. They were from Louisville and gave Karen and me so much support both of the times we were there.

Things were financially pretty tight and crazily busy. I would pull a night shift as a front desk clerk at Fairfield Inn. Then I would leave there to deliver about 300 newspapers on a paper route (sometimes accompanied by one of my kids) before heading to classes. After classes, I would teach a couple of subjects at a small Christian school before going home for dinner. I would try to squeeze in some time with the family, then do it all over again. When I finally walked across the platform of the Alumni Chapel to get my diploma, I wept tears of joyous release. Up to that time, it was the greatest sense of personal accomplishment I had ever felt.

By the way, just as Dr. Honeycutt warned, the seminary was eventually taken over by the fundamentalists. When Dr. Al Mohler became president, there was a purge of liberal professors, and the social work program was disbanded. It was a completely different regime my second time there. Under both leaders, however, I received a quality education by highly qualified professors who really cared about their students. I just wish it didn't have to be that way.

I have served the church and community with one foot firmly planted in two disparagingly different worlds: social work and ministry, liberal and conservative, government and church, secular and sacred. Theologically, I consider myself a conservative. Some would call me a fundamentalist, probably as a slur. Pragmatically, I consider myself a moderate. Some would call me a liberal, also as a slur. I'm just trying to stay balanced between the guiding principles of truth and grace. My goal is to be fully empowered by both. It's not truth *or* grace. It's truth *and* grace. I believe error always comes in pairs of opposites. Our ancient enemy loves to keep us on either extreme, fighting one another.

After all of that effort and energy to get my divinity degree, I ultimately ended up back in social work. Go figure. Doing things out of order appears to be a pattern, if not the major thesis, of my life. More on that coming up.

Ever make a mistake? Sure you have. If you are anything like me, you've made plenty. But here's another question. Have you ever made a divinely inspired mistake? In other words, have you ever made a mistake that has God's providential fingerprints all over it? Because the Lord "makes all things work to the good for those who love Him and are called according to His purposes," our blunders often look like they were part of God's divine plan, as if He orchestrated our failures for our own good.

Here's what I have learned about that: those mistakes don't work for our good unless, and until, we acknowledge them as failures on our part. Not only must we own our failures, we must also work hard toward not making the same mistakes again. Only then will we see anything positive come from the messes we make. When we do wrong, and confess it as such, God immediately begins to make it right. That's amazing, and it's called Grace.

While I believe it was wrong to leave Alliance Bible Church, especially under such unnecessary circumstances, I'm even more convinced it was a divinely inspired mistake. I should have stayed. I should have taken the criticism. I should have adjusted my attitude and grown into my position. I should have done a lot of things differently, but I didn't. My ten-year-old self would say, "Shoulda. Coulda. Woulda."

The late Dr. Adrian Rogers once asked a simple question that best explains what I mean by a divinely inspired mistake: "Has it ever occurred to you that nothing has ever occurred to God?" The sovereignty of God means absolutely nothing if our slip-ups catch him off guard, if our stubbornness to do His will forces Him to change his plans, or if our sinfulness thwarts His holy desires. In my flesh I was wrong to leave. In God's divine plan for me, it all worked for the good. So relax. God's got you.

Bottom Line: Sincerity is a fine art, and well worth the high price to obtain it. Transparency is healthy. Reckless honesty, on the other hand, is not.

6
Reproved

Change has no natural constituencies except those who are desperate.

A LIST OF THE TOP FIVE most often played songs on my iTunes reveals something about me:

5. *Bring Me to Life* by Evanescence

4. *Owner of a Lonely Heart* by Yes

3. *The Pretender* by Foo Fighters

2. *Bad Blood* by Bastille

1. *In the End* by LINKIN PARK

Can you see any similarity (or hear any, as the case may be)? My kids wisecrack answer: "Yea, Dad, they're ancient." Although I am fond of the classic hard rock sound, it's not age, or beat, they have in common. It's message. Themes of anger, angst, alienation, conflict, and yearning seem to speak to me. Each tune could easily be a chapter heading in my life story. The most listened to in my musical collection, however, probably best summarizes this chapter, the chorus in particular.

Released in 2001, "In the End" represented my life for nearly a decade; so much so, I have asked my family to play it at my funeral. Yes, I'm serious about that.

I tried so hard
And got so far
But in the end
It doesn't even matter
I had to fall to lose it all
But in the end it doesn't even matter

It reminds me of the core theme running through the book of Ecclesiastes: life is little more than vanity and chasing after the wind. I don't recommend reading it while depressed. However, I think the book is very liberating if the message is unashamedly embraced. It can actually set the reader free from a great deal of burden. According to the Preacher, success doesn't matter. Neither does failure. Think about it. That is the formula for freedom. I have inadvertently tested his theory at many junctures in my life and found it to be true. When I am able to lean into the security of that divine truth, all worry and anxiety disappear.

That is the true peace that surpasses all understanding!

Try to look at it this way. Worry is undue concern about what did, or didn't, happen in the past. Anxiety is undue concern about what might, or might not, happen in the future. Since Jesus has our past and our future covered, and since success or failure doesn't really matter in the end, there simply isn't any cause for those twin troubles of the heart to have any influence in our lives.

Let me tell you now about an intensely deep layer of the onion I had to peel away in order to get to that sweet spot. I'm not saying I stay there, but I have been there on occasion, and it is marvelous.

After graduation from Southern Seminary the second time, I pastored a small country church for about a year. It was actually my home church, Newcomb Baptist, where I was saved and called to the ministry. I did not follow the money, but instead followed the Lord's calling to pastor a smaller church.

An even stranger twist of fate, Uncle Don, brother to my foster mother (Mom Ball), was the interim pastor. Uncle Don was the shepherd of the little church that played such a critical role in my early spiritual development. He unexpectedly passed away not long after I took the position, but I had enough time to reconnect with him and learn more about the time I spent in my first foster home.

He also revealed something I did not know. When I was in college, I had applied for a part-time youth ministry position. I was confident I would be offered the job. They had nearly said as much. At the last minute, though, they decided to go with another candidate. I thought something was odd but didn't give it much more thought. I was soon busy starting Mountain Outreach and thought it simply the bigger plan of God. Uncle Don told me what happened and why I was ultimately rejected for the position. Someone told the search committee who my mother was, and the church leadership decided they could not hire someone with "that kind of background." It was not the first, nor would it be the last, time I was discriminated against because of my family.

It was while I was at Newcomb that I was reunited with my four brothers, 28 years after we were separated as children. I was also reconnected with Aunt Moe and Aunt Sweetheart, who had loved and cared for me during eight years of my childhood, when my mother wouldn't. The short tenure at my home church seemed to be more about self-discovery and restoration of things lost than it was about leading a congregation.

Returning to the area was kind of surreal. I was back, but I wasn't home. The place and the people were pretty much the same, but I was different. They were proud of the boy preacher who came back home to pastor. I was honored to serve the people who had loved me and had given me a chance. But we both felt it wasn't the same as before, nor was it what either of us expected. How could it have been? I left a church in Alaska because I didn't feel like I belonged, and eventually returned to my home church only to feel the same way. I was a man without a culture, a home, or sense of well-being.

Newcomb, Tennessee, was once a thriving coal town with its own train station. It had long since become a mere shadow of its former self. Unincorporated, it was really just an extension of Jellico. Jerry's Market was the center of the community, and the owners were its heartbeat. A good portion of the population drew a government-issued check. My yankee wife stuck out like a sore thumb.

Karen didn't understand why everyone sat on their front porches in the evenings, sometimes all day. She liked to walk, which wasn't exactly an unknown sight in the community, but Karen would always take our dog, who would be on a leash. People around there just didn't do that. Dogs weren't on leashes. Plus, why would a dog need to be walked? One day she was passing a neighbor who was sitting on his porch as usual. He made a statement that had probably been the subject of conversation by the locals gathered over at Jerry's Market: "Ma'am, you're go'n to walk dat poor dog to death."

The residents of Newcomb also thought she kept the prettiest garden they'd ever seen. It wasn't really a compliment, though. They didn't see any practical use for a good-looking garden. Karen once asked the ladies at church how to grow green tomatoes. They chuckled and someone asked, "Do you have any tomato plants in your garden?" She proudly said, "Yes, 21." With a slight look of amazement, someone replied, "Then honey, just pick 'em before they turn red." I still love to tease her about that.

After about three months, some of the members were beginning to question what had happened to me. Boo Boo, one of the deacons (he and his wife Girdie are about the nicest people you'll ever meet anywhere), with a wad of chewing tobacco between his cheek and gums confessed to me, "I've been wait'n the longest time for you to do some real preach'n, you know, like ya use to. I don't reckon you're ever gonna either. But that's alright. I want ya to know, I've learnt more about the Bible in the short time you've been here than I ever learnt from all the rest of them preachers put together." It was the most gratifying compliment I have received from a parishioner.

For the year I was there, I tried to develop a relationship with my mother, who lived only a few miles away. We had not talked for the ten years I was in Alaska, but she seemed excited about getting reconnected. She had not met three of my children. At first she appeared delighted to get to know her grandbabies, but I was hesitant and shielded them until I could see how it was going to go. We would visit her and her fourth husband, Richard Wendel, at their house. Sometimes we'd pick blackberries from the briar patches in their yard.

For some reason she would never visit us. I did finally manage to get her to agree to spend Thanksgiving together at our home. I was disappointed, but not surprised, when she called moments before the meal was ready to say she wasn't feeling well and couldn't come. Karen put a plate of food together and suggested I take it to them so they would have something to eat, and they would know we were trying to make the relationship work. When I arrived with the food, I discovered my mother had friends over. They had been drinking since early that morning. Despite being hurt by another act of rejection, I attempted to stay in touch while I remained in Newcomb. She pretty much stopped trying altogether. Eventually, I did too.

With the congregation's blessing, I moved on about the time of my one-year anniversary. It was shortly after the fizzle of Y2K. We both knew it wasn't going to work in the long term, and we didn't want to get cross with one another. It was a positive and friendly departure. From there I went to work at my alma mater, Cumberland College, just as I had done so many years before as a novice believer. This time I went to teach rather than to learn. I had already been doing some adjunct instruction for the school while pastoring, but they wanted me to go full time. I thought it was a chance of a lifetime and was deeply honored by the offer.

The first time I left the church I was 18 and the deacons warned, "That college will ruin you." This time I was 38 and they warned, "That college will fire you." They were prophetic once again.

Being a founder of Mountain Outreach, I was the poster child for the college. The program had proved to be a big boon: more students, more donors, more recognition, and lots of goodwill. For that contribution they had inducted me into the Alumni Hall of Honor in 1995. Returning as an Assistant Professor of Social Work was something that seemed to benefit us both.

Side note: the director of Mountain Outreach turned out to be my cousin. We may have met once as children but neither of us is certain. I discovered we were related when I visited the offices to check in with the ministry I helped build. There were pictures of families on the wall who had just received a new house. One was of my aunt, who is two years younger than me. I hadn't seen her in many years but recognized the Wood family resemblance. I commented, "Looks like you guys built a house for my aunt." The secretary responded, "Then our new director must be your cousin." We met and discovered it was true. He was the son of one of my mother's younger sisters. She married when she was only 13. Despite poverty and struggles of his own, Will Jones has done exceedingly well for himself. Currently, he is the president of Bethany College in Kansas. I am very proud of him. Another one of Sophia's grandchildren made it out alive and well. If you read my first book, *Worst of Mother's…Best of Moms*, you know that's saying something.

Actually, I had predicted returning to Cumberland College three years earlier. I recorded in my journal that the Lord had impressed upon me I would one day return there to teach. I had no clue at the time when, or how, it would ever take place, and yet it did. He didn't tell me in advance, though, how it was going to end. It was the turn of the new century, and I had landed my dream job. It wasn't just the job, but the place itself. I was teaching at the setting where, as a poor kid, I first starting dreaming of doing better.

---

499. The Fire

Have you ever thought about how much we owe to sorrow and suffering? Perhaps you have never stopped to consider that tribulation has produced some of the greatest written works of mankind. Most of the Psalms, for example, were born in a wilderness experience. Most of the New Testament letters were written in prison.

Even outside of the Bible, suffering has created enduring publications that have become the mainstream of Christian hope and encouragement. The best thoughts of some of our greatest thinkers have passed through the fiery furnace. So many composers of our favorite hymns learned in suffering what they taught us in song. It was in bonds that Bunyan lived the allegory that he afterwards penned. We can thank his chains for that Pilgrim's Progress.

So, take comfort my afflicted Christian friends. When God is about to make preeminent use of a man or woman, He turns up the heat. He puts pressure on his vessel, and squeezes out of them precious works of art.

StraightTalkwithRobertDay.com

I tried so hard, and I'd come so far, but in the end, it didn't even matter.

I loved being a teacher. According to my student evaluations, I was pretty good at it. I got personally involved in many of their activities and events outside the classroom. My Introduction to Sociology course was pretty popular. We had to keep adding additional classes each semester to meet the demand. Out of respect, they called me Mr. Day. Of course, it's expected that students formally address their instructors from kindergarten through college that way, but I felt special every time I heard it. In my childhood, people with such titles were the only decent people I knew. I carried Mr. like a badge of honor.

The seventh, and last, church I served was one I started in the living room of my home. Many of the students attended. It was another avenue for ministry to them. It helped that our service started at 2:00 pm on Sundays. They could sleep in and still go to church. The congregation grew and we started meeting in a Seventh Day Adventist church. As churches go, we were a bit odd. People could ask questions during the sermon. We spent time sharing testimonies and praying for one another. We focused on the Scriptures, Service, and Sharing. Nearly every member was actively involved in a ministry outside the church, something we stressed and celebrated all the time. Since the church had few expenses, most of the income from the offerings was distributed to numerous missionary causes. The years I voluntarily pastored that small congregation were filled with joy and contentment, in large part because of the college kids. My family still fondly remembers many of them. It was a pleasure to lead that church.

For the first time in my ministry, I was free to be me. There was no pressure to be anything other than myself. I was not paid a salary. I did not need or want one. There is something liberating about leading a group of people you are not dependent on to feed your family and pay your bills. There was no denominational box into which I was forced to fit, nor were there unrealistic expectations, or demands, about keeping tradition or growing a church for the sake of church growth. I allowed, and was allowed, authenticity, truthfulness, and freedom to try out different approaches to ministry. That removed the stress to perform, to succeed, or to do what had always been done.

In the fall of 2003, the student body awarded me and another teacher The Most Honored Professor Award. Besides the recognition itself, and an accompanying plaque for our office walls, we were the grand marshals for the annual Homecoming Parade. I would have been happy teaching and mentoring those young people the rest of my life. Within a couple of weeks, however, right in the middle of the semester, I was no longer employed. I was fired. They said I resigned. In reality it was a forced resignation, what they call in Human Resources a "constructive termination."

I had to fall, to lose it all, but in the end, it didn't even matter.

The internet's free collaborative encyclopedia, *Wikipedia*, maintains a University of the Cumberland page. Under the heading "Controversies," there is a section titled Robert Day.

In 2003, the American Association of University Professors (AAUP) found that President Taylor coerced Professor Robert Day into resigning because he had opposed Taylor's proposed staff layoffs on an off-campus website. The AAUP concluded that "The policies of Cumberland College, including the grievance procedure, do not provide for faculty hearings of any kind. College policies and practices preclude any effective faculty role in academic governance and contribute to an atmosphere that stifles the freedom of faculty to question and criticize administrative decisions and actions." The AAUP noted that current and former faculty members "do not feel free to address topics of college concern in any forum" and "described a climate of fear about what faculty members may say and do, a fear based on what they know or have been told has happened to others." Those interviewed "expressed a particular fear that criticizing the administration and its operation of the college could place a faculty member's appointment in jeopardy."

It's a long story, and I'm not willing to discuss all the details here because it doesn't serve any purpose. Suffice it to say, both sides were wrong, but I freely admit I started it. I thought I was battling an injustice, something people coming out of my kind of situation often have a hypersensitivity against. That certainly was a factor.

In truth, though, the AAUP didn't have access to what was going on in my mind and heart at the time. Not only was I combating a perceived injustice, I was also fighting my way out of a familiar corner that success, and the feelings of rejection, had once again painted me into. It was probably even more than that. In the spirit of full disclosure, I was probably subconsciously getting revenge on President Taylor.

Mountain Outreach built its 100th house in the fall of 2002. The college wanted to take that opportunity to celebrate and get some positive publicity. Being a co-founder, I was originally slated to be a speaker at the event. As the date drew closer, the administration decided there were too many speakers and the program needed to be shortened. I was asked to give the closing prayer instead. To be honest, I was a little put off. However, I agreed. I was a part of the Cumberland family and wanted to do what was best for the school. Then the week before the event, I was informed I would not even be offering a prayer. The main speaker was E.H. Hutton, the brother of the more famous E.F. Hutton. He was a major donor to the college and had several things on campus bearing his name. Mr. Hutton was an atheist, and Dr. Taylor was first concerned my speech would offend the VIP. Later he worried my prayer would as well, so I was taken off the program entirely. At Cumberland, when E.H. Hutton spoke, Dr. Taylor listened. I was assured, though, I could attend if I wanted. I didn't.

When I was a student, I spent countless hours to make that program successful. I passed up many opportunities, missed a lot of fun, and worked nearly every weekend for three years to birth and build the ministry. At first I was discouraged by the administration, and in some ways hampered by them. Later, I was used by the same administration to raise funds for the college. I was a poor kid from the mountains, and I was building houses for the poor. They ate that up at the New York Yacht club. In the years to follow, the college milked Mountain Outreach for all they could. But now as a staff member, I had no clout, no hook, nothing to be exploited. In fact, they thought I might get in the way.

Once again rejection triggered the worst in me.

Being told I could not participate in the thing I started bothered me more than I let on. Later, when the administration started laying off a large number of employees, I became incensed. Most of them got notice of their termination by email, with a notice to vacate their offices in one hour. I felt like those who sacrificed for the college were being treated poorly. It was a pattern I had seen many times over the years, starting when I was a student. Since the college was in the middle of several building projects, it appeared to me to be a cruel injustice. When I publicly, but not very professionally, called out the administration, I was terminated. The rest is history worth an entire paragraph on the internet (sarcasm font).

By this time it had become painfully obvious to me there was a destructive pattern in my life and I needed to change, or it would likely repeat again. This particular incident was extremely difficult on my wife and kids. If for no other reason than for them, I had to break this maladaptive pattern.

Some people reading this may come to the conclusion I'm just "some kind of special stupid." They may be right. I'll grant them that. It is, indeed, some kind of really empty-headed thinking that causes people like myself to continually self-destruct. Yet it isn't all that unusual. It's far too common, in fact. Consider the battered woman who always goes back to her abuser. Ponder for a moment the man who loses so much to alcohol or drugs and keeps on with his addiction despite the high personal cost. Think about the individuals who can't keep friends for long because of the drama they continually bring to every relationship. Those behaviors are stupid for sure. The people aren't necessarily so. They are likely just living according to a script that's running, unchecked, from their gut to their heads.

It's like computer software operating in their brain, except the program was written by a hurting child. It's supremely powerful. It can make adults do really idiotic stuff. Past hurt is often reciprocal. Hurt causes hurt, and the effects of hurt add up. Nonetheless, the code can be rewritten, secure attachments can be found, and the outcomes can be altered, not merely redirected. The good news is that mental malware can be wiped cleaned. The gospel provides a clean slate and enables a fresh start. It is the only thing that can.

Trauma, neglect, dysfunctional lifestyles, and unproductive behaviors learned in childhood will always show their worst negative effects later in adulthood. Just like unhealed wounds can fester and spread their infection to other parts of the body, emotional injuries can become hotbeds of psychological disorders and diseases. A child growing up in an emotionally toxic home, for example, may learn to survive by not talking, not trusting, and not feeling. Children may grow up learning to lie in order to survive. Lying becomes so ingrained by the time they are adults, deception is truth. What worked well as a kid, though, can cause severe damage as an adult. The stakes are much higher. Those behaviors served the child well in that environment and at that time in their life, but later it will be like an improvised explosive device (IED) hidden deep within them. They'll be driving down the road, so to speak, in another time and a different setting and something will trigger the explosion. The aftermath can be devastating for anyone in close proximity.

So how does someone change something that is so deeply rooted in them? How does a wounded person transform their inner pain rather than transmit it to others or destroy themselves?

Here's the thing about that: change has no natural constituencies except those who are desperate. That idea is not original to me. I've undoubtedly remembered it because it so clearly communicates the proposition of this chapter, even this book. If it is true, then it stands to reason that the forces for change must be greater than the forces against change. Desperation and despair are the precious resources that fuel most, if not all, change. The Scriptures and stories of the Bible scream two consistent messages throughout the inspired pages. First, there is no growth without struggle. Secondly, there is no transformation without suffering.

The Lord made sure I would finally become desperate or hopeless enough to break that negative cycle once and for all. My Heavenly Teacher, my Divine Counselor, my Eternal Father, took me through seven years of wilderness wanderings in order to complete the good work he started in me. If I were a superstitious man, I would have thought I had broken a mirror somewhere. Throughout that period of my life, He continued to love me and care for my family. There were times I was unemployed, or underemployed, but we never did without what was truly needed. There were occasions I had to work two or three jobs at a time to make ends meet, but we managed. The entire time I never felt at peace with the work I was doing, nor did I really have much success. In the course of that dispensation, I never thought I was doing what God had called me to do. I did what was necessary, but never did I feel I was doing the extraordinary.

Throughout my nearly a decade of vanity and striving after the wind, I did many things that in the end didn't matter. I was part of a group that started a Christian camp. It lasted one summer before closing. Along with a business partner, I opened a wholesale Christian book business. It went bankrupt a year later. I did sales for a tech company, but never closed a single deal. The owner kept me on for a while as a charity case. Not everything was a failure, though. I was adjunct instructor in the Social Work department at Eastern Kentucky University. The longest job I had during this period was as the Technical Consultant for First Steps, Kentucky's early intervention program. But even those jobs seemed like spot holders, like I was just biding my time.

In one interval of unemployment, I powerwashed for a couple of weeks. I needed the cash, so from sunrise to sunset I sprayed the mold, dirt, and dog poop off the walkways and decks of a group of cheap apartment complexes. I'd be soaked at the end of the day and pondering how I ended up there. It's not that I felt above the task. I was not afraid of manual labor. I've done my fair share over the years. It's just not what I thought I was meant to do. At the end of one remarkably depressing day, covered in nasty, wet stew from head to toe, I prayed a little prayer. "Lord, if this is your will for my life, then so be it." Then I countered, "But it's not what you told me it would be. Please continue to wash away all the mess in my life that's keeping me from doing what you promised."

I felt so far off the original path that God had set for me, I thought I would never get back on track. Now equipped with the vision that accompanies looking back, I see the Lord had a purpose for everything that occurred in those refining years. He was teaching, guiding, and healing me with each and every step. What appeared to me as being off the divine trail, and nothing more than a series of unrelated jobs, was actually a specially prepared road God had constructed just for me. It was my own personal transformation workout, if you will. He was preparing me for the promise.

The Potter didn't just use jobs, or lack thereof, to press and form His clay vessel those seven lean years. My health was impaired as well. I struggled with some strange kind of illness that zapped my energy and left me with odd body aches. One local doctor called it a "mystery wrapped in an enigma." A trip to the Mayo clinic put us on the tract of Lyme disease. My youngest daughter was diagnosed with anorexia nervosa. On two separate occasions, her weight became so dangerously low we were close to hospitalizing her so she could be tube fed. In that same year, Karen's sister Heather fought a battle with cancer and lost. The woman who worked so hard to keep our family together was gone for a good part of a year helping to care for her sister. That put a lot of stress on the entire family. On top of all that, our basement flooded. Twice! It cost money we didn't have. Through every corrective experience, though, the Lord sustained my family and changed me.

Here's a crucial life lesson I learned from all of that crazy stuff: how things look, and how things feel, are often not how things are. Dear friends, listen to me. Don't trust your perceptions. Don't trust your feelings. Don't trust your circumstances. Trust God's promises instead. Because how things are in any given moment is not His purpose for you.

I tried so hard and got so far. But in the end, it didn't even matter. I had to fall to lose it all. But in the end, it didn't even matter.

Bottom Line: If you don't transform your pain, you will transmit it, and there will be unwanted, and maybe even irreversible, damage.

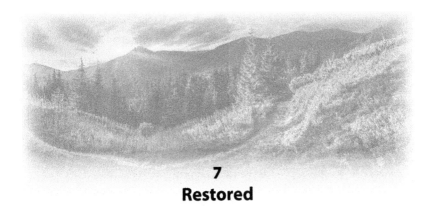

7
Restored

The torture to stay must become worse than the torment to leave.

D EPENDING ON HOW YOU LOOK AT IT, there are three or four steps (or stages) in the healing process. These stages are referred to by many different terms as they are viewed through the colored lenses of various authorities: psychology, sociology, philosophy, or theology. These various phases seem to be universally recognized to some extent, although maybe not completely understood. Because they are such an integral part of the human story, we see them in nearly every novel and movie. You'll certainly find them throughout the pages of the Bible, the greatest story ever told. The following is my version of the process.

Stage One — The Problem. We all have at least one, and probably more. We usually don't pick them. They pick us. Remember, we started out being a part of someone else's story and suffered the collateral damage from their problem. I was part of the drama of my mother's life and a victim of her many bad decisions. I was born into sin, raised in a fallen culture, inherited her pain, suffered from her problems, and caused plenty of my own. In time, with habitual practice, her troubles became normal patterns in my own life. The biblical description of "the sins of the fathers (and mothers) being visited upon the children" is accurate.

The challenge of this first step of the process is to name the problem (or the sin) and own it as our own. That's easier said than done. It's very hard to be honest with ourselves, and we don't much like it when others point out the obvious. Yet that is exactly what must take place. It is the starting line.

Stage Two — The Pressure. Like a dog that returns to its vomit, we would continue to remain in our problem if there was no pressure to do otherwise. Since we grew up with it, we have learned to live with our problem, and to some degree, even use it to our advantage. Much like the theory of evolution, we adapted in order to survive in our world. We are tempted to keep a tight grip on our adaptive behaviors because they have been useful in some way or another. Some children learn early to lie, for example, in order to survive. After a while, lying becomes second nature, and they can no longer distinguish truth from a falsehood.

The goal of this level is to recognize the need for change. That won't likely happen without some strong external pressure forcing the issue. Fortunately for us, one advantage of living in a fallen world is that everything eventually stops working, even our excuses.

Stage Three — The Pain. Pain can be an excellent teacher if we allow it. No pain, no gain, the saying goes. In this stage we must become so uncomfortable with our beloved problem, with our cherished sin, that we are motivated to take steps away from it and into the unknown future without it. This is a tough phase. People don't fear change as much as they fear loss, especially if it is the loss of a familiar, yet destructive, problem. It is painful to stay in the problem, and it is painful to get out. The torture to stay must become worse than the torment to leave.

Some people may refer to this step as "hitting rock bottom." I'm not sure that's the same, however. My brother Randy was certainly at the bottom. He was there a long time. He lost everything, but for some reason never felt motivated to change.

Stage Four—The Peace. Our final destination is a new normal. It's a position of peace where our past and our problems are no longer in control of our lives. Because this is uncharted territory, it's usually uncomfortable at first. We will likely step in and out of that peaceful place several times before deciding to take up residence. If you grow up only knowing war, declaring peace can be frightening. We know we have a new emotional address in this phase when we have a new nature, free of the power of our former problem/sin.

None of these steps is easy. They all have their own timing and pace, but this final one will likely take much longer than any of us wants. It's a matter of sin as much as it is an issue with past hurt that keeps us from getting there sooner. That is why spiritual formation must be a part of emotional healing.

While it is possible to go through the entire process of all four stages without the aid of human help, I strongly recommend seeking Christian counseling to provide guidance and support. Patrick Henry Family Services has long appreciated the value of counseling when working with children and families. Our Hope for Tomorrow Counseling centers provide professional, Christian counseling built on solid biblical principles. Our licensed counselors understand the natural process of change:

a. Your experience has caused you to believe the wrong things.
b. Those beliefs are hurting you, and will continue to hurt you, as well as those around you.
c. Changing will be tough, but it will make it better.
d. Don't abandon the process until it does get better. I'll be here for you.

The last two years of my seven-year transformational journey I spent in northern Indiana working as a major gift officer for Goshen College, a Mennonite school. Never in a thousand years would I have ever guessed I would be there, doing that. I desperately needed the job and was grateful for it. I owe a debt of gratitude to my boss, Jim Caskey, for giving me the opportunity, and for demonstrating how raising money can, and should, be performed as a ministry.

While it was a great pleasure to serve in that capacity, it seemed like I had traveled so far away from the will of God. Unknown to me at the time, in the two short years I spent there I would learn important skills and gain valuable experience that made it possible for me to have the amazing job I have now. The real benefit, though, is something I could not have imagined. In an open letter published in the campus newspaper, I wrote about my sojourn there and what it had done for me:

> I have long admired Mennonites from a distance. And for the last two years I have had the wonderful privilege of living and working among them to test the merit of that admiration. I am happy to report that this closer proximity to Mennonites has been thoroughly educational and even deeply therapeutic.
>
> There are many things about the Mennonite faith, culture and ethos I wish I had been blessed with earlier in my life. So much so that the last two years felt like I had been in mourning over the loss of what most Mennonites seem to take for granted: the abiding ties of family, the beauty of simplicity, the security of order, the joy of generosity, and a culture for service.

In short, the peace-centered community of anabaptists helped me walk into Stage Four, that position of inner peace, and motivated me to stay there. It wasn't anything intentional that anybody did. It was simply working and living there that God used to bring about a fuller healing.

As my job required, I visited alumni and donors of the college all across Illinois, Indiana, Ohio, Michigan, and Pennsylvania. One trip included several states all across the South. I sat in the homes of people I didn't know existed: healthy, prosperous, hospitable, gracious, and kindhearted people with solid families. Every person I met on my travels possessed global perspectives, held deep convictions, and abided in a genuine faith. Just being amongst them helped me to yearn for the peace they seemed to possess naturally.

It was while I was living in Goshen my mother passed away. The timing of that seemed to put final closure on my childhood. The next chapter of my life began, and my years of wandering finally came to an end. There is no way to describe it other than to say I was free. The death of my mother loosed me of a burden I had borne for far too long.

It was nothing I did, nor the fault of the college, that I and a number of people were laid off. It was the consequence of the Great Recession. In stark contrast to the administration at Cumberland College, I was told in person and given 30 days notice. I was also provided the option to take the rest of the day off in order to process the news. I spent my time off that day on the internet looking for work. It was something I'd grown accustomed to doing. Within just a few minutes of being logged onto ChristianJobs.org, I saw a posting for the Executive Director of a children's home in Virginia. It was the first day it was posted. I immediately applied, and my résumé was the first they received. After a couple of phone interviews, and a visit to the organization, I was hired. My last day at Goshen college was on a Friday, 30 days later. My first day on the new job was on the following Monday, June 1, 2010. I didn't miss a paycheck in between moves. I was 49, and I sensed things were finally turning around.

Not only did God have a good "job" waiting, He had the perfect "ministry" prepared for me. He had orchestrated the expedition of the past seven years. He had carefully timed each stage and guided every step. What I had thought was a series of misfortunate events, or the consequences of my poor choices, was really the Lord working all things for the good. He had arranged a healing regimen that put me perfectly in the center of His will.

I have now been at Patrick Henry Family Services for a little more than seven years. That's longer than my wilderness wandering. I have continued to grow, learn, and improve. I have been blessed beyond measure and feel I am a fortunate individual. I've enjoyed more peace, prosperity, and success there than ever in my life. God is doing something extraordinary in this organization, and I'm very pleased to be a part of it. More on that in the next book.

No matter what mess or pain you are in today, I want you to know something: the cause of that mess, the cause of that pain, is not decisive in explaining them. The cause doesn't matter. Certainly there are causes. Some of those causes may be your own fault. Some of them may be the fault of others. And some are simply the result of living in a fallen world. It rains on the just and unjust alike. The point is this: in God's Kingdom, it's the purpose for the pain, not the cause of the pain, on which we must focus.

Romans 8:28 tells us that "all things work together for those who love God and are called according to His purposes." Did you get that...according to His purposes. John Piper teaches that none of the mess or pain makes any sense; none of it is helpful "if God Himself, and the glory of His works, is not our greatest treasure."

Whatever layer needs to be peeled back for you, whatever the process might look like in your particular situation, there is something you must do. Since you can't do it by yourself, you need help. Professional help is good. I cannot recommend it enough. It would have saved me a great deal of trouble. A Christian counselor can smooth out the bumpy parts of the journey, hold a mirror up to you, and hear your secrets without judgment.

At the same time, you need to pick others to help you as well. People who will walk with you and not just talk to you. You need to find the kind of people you want to become. They need to operate like a family to you, who can help you learn to trust again. Few can heal from the effects of trauma without the support of a family network. This is especially true when the trauma came from the context of family. Ask them to go with you through the stages and hold you accountable at each step. Find quality individuals who will kick your butt if you don't go to counseling and follow the plan. Warning: it may not be any of your friends. They could be part of the problem. You need people who are healthy themselves. Look for the people you needed when you were younger and ask them to help you to be that person now.

---

543. Two Levels

There are two levels of faith. There's the level that says we know God can answer our prayers. We believe He has the power, and we trust He'll answer in His time.

But there is a deeper level. It's the kind of faith that says I believe God will change ME so that I will be OK if He doesn't make the changes I'm requesting. It's faith that believes, even when God doesn't do the things we ask. We continue to ask, knowing He has the power to answer our prayers. We rely on HIS wisdom and HIS power to protect, strengthen, and comfort, even when we don't see answers, even if things never change, even when things aren't going our way.

I spent years living in the first level. It's not a bad place. But I think the second level is a better place. I'm not always worrying about how, or when, God will answer my prayers.... I live in the assurance He has it under control.

StraightTalkwithRobertDay.org

Special Thanks to Claudia Fletcher for the inspiration for this segment. Check out her blog Never a Dull Moment at http://fletcherclan. blogspot.com/

Here is another bit of advice. It's going to be difficult to follow. It may, however, be the most critical decision in your process of getting better. You may have to cut all ties with your family of origin, or at least erect a barrier between them and you. You may also have to walk away from your culture in order to get well. Let me explain.

In *Worst of Mothers... Best of Moms,* I wrote about my brother Joe and his suicide about a year after our mother's death. Then, just about the time that book was going to press, I learned my brother Randy had died. No one knows the cause of his death. The police found his body in a dumpster (or storage container) in Texas, hundreds of miles from where he was last seen by family in Iowa. The information isn't clear. They believe he'd been there for some time before being discovered. I do know Randy had a major substance abuse problem. He had lost all his teeth from using meth, and was living under a bridge when last I heard.

As a little boy, he was the cutest of us five boys. My second to youngest brother had a winsome personality that managed to shine even through all the damage of drugs and alcohol. He was also the wildest of the bunch.

One Sunday we were heading back home from church when I got a frantic call from my oldest daughter who had stayed home sick that morning. With a little bit of panic she said, "Dad, there's a homeless man banging on the doors and looking through the windows. What should I do?" I told her to stay calm and remain hiding in her closet. We were only a couple of minutes away, and from the physical description she gave me, I had a suspicion it was one of my brothers.

Sure enough, there was my brother Randy with a big toothless grin on his grimy face as we pulled into the driveway. Karen and the kids went in the house as I talked to him. He reported he had hitchhiked from Iowa to our "ole Kentucky home." The description of life on the road and the vile things he had to do in order to eat and get rides was disgusting, to say the least. Nevertheless, he told it in a matter-of-fact tone, as if everyone did those kinds of things when they traveled. After we hugged, I asked him, "What are you doing here, Randy?"

"I've come to stay with you, big brother."

"Why did you do that?"

"'Cause I thought you could help me."

"Help you with what, little brother?"

"Get my shit together, man."

He went on to explain he wanted to be sober and clean so he could get a job. Well, that sounded promising and all, but I had serious doubts. I brought him inside the house and let him take a shower while I washed his filthy clothes. Then we fed him some dinner and visited for a while. I eventually told him I could not let him stay in my home. He was happy to just camp out in the backyard for as long as it took. It would undoubtedly be a better situation than the kind of places he was used to living in. Moreover, my family didn't feel comfortable, and we were fostering at the time. There was no way he was going to pass a background check.

At any rate, I still would not have let him stay with us. Years ago I decided I had to build some boundaries, a firewall if you will, between my dysfunctional family and my own wife and kids. It was part of my promise they would not experience the things I did growing up.

I put him up in a motel for three days while I tried to talk him into going to rehab. It took that long to research the options and make the arrangements. I was willing to pay what I could in order to get him admitted, and I was more than willing to assist him when he got out. On the third day, though, he was drunk out of his mind. It was sadly obvious to me he was not serious. The next day I drove him sixty miles down the interstate and dropped him off so he could return to Iowa, or wherever he wanted to go. I wanted some distance between him and my family. I gave him some money for food, but not much because I feared he would use it instead on a binge.

Did I feel bad about it? Yes, sure I did. Was I to blame for his addiction? No, not one bit. Was I responsible for his recovery? Nope. Should I have done more? Maybe, but I don't think so.

Some might think me cruel. Others may consider what I did unchristian. I believe it was wisdom and the ultimate act of kindness to my own family. When Jesus said that we (His followers) would have to leave mother and father, brother and sister to follow Him, I think this is the kind of thing He was talking about. We can choose health and wholeness in Him, or we can stay captive and sick with our broken and dysfunctional families. We should always hold out hope they will break free. We should never stop praying they will find the Lord. We should always be ready to help where, and when, it is sensible and safe.

I hail from a culture that places a high value on family. That is one of the strengths of the mountain people. There are no ties stronger than family in those hills and hollows. Unfortunately, it's also their weakness. I have seen, for example, an elderly grandmother use her entire tiny savings for bail money to get her drug-addicted adult grandchild out of jail, only to be robbed and beaten later by the same ungrateful punk. Then weeks later, she allowed the same sorry kin to move in with her because he had nowhere else to go. That's what "good, loving families do," was her reasoning.

Friends, please listen to me on this point. Either let go or get dragged. You are not being disloyal, or selfish, or unkind by saying no and walking away. You are choosing to be healthy. I'll come to the aid of anyone who needs it and wants it. It has nothing to do with being deserving or undeserving. Everyone is deserving of help. It doesn't matter what they've done. They are created in the image of God, and that makes them worthy. I'm unwilling, however, to help anybody stay in their problem, or enable them to hurt others with their problem. My personal compassion manifesto is clear on this matter. I refuse to empower anyone's dysfunction and destruction—even those in my family.

Two of my four maternal half-brothers have now lost their lives tragically, far too many years before their time. All four have had difficulties as adults. Between them, they have struggled with substance abuse, crime, chronic unemployment, multiple failed relationships, and unsupported children. When we were permanently separated as kids, I thought they were the lucky ones — they had a good life, and they had their dad. I was the one left with our crazy mother, with no father. They returned to Iowa, the place I idealized in my mind as opposite of where I was and how I was being treated.

Growing up, I believed they were all right, leading "normal" lives. It ended up not being the case. They grew up thinking I had a bad life, which was mostly true. If you consider the cards I was dealt, I could easily be the one living under the bridge. I could be the one with multiple failed marriages. I could be the one with an alcohol problem. I could be the one consistently out of work. I could, but I'm not. Why? Well, that is the point of this book, and I hope you have gleaned the difference from my story.

In summary, there are at least two broad reasons.

1. Despite a childhood of poverty and abuse, I had some good people who were actively involved in my rescue. There were many Christian people praying for me, helping me, influencing me, providing opportunities for me. Though inconsistent, church was a part of my life. My brothers didn't have that. For more, read *Worst of Mothers... Best of Moms*.

2. As an adult, I've made some good choices. I made critical decisions at the right times, and took many important steps that liberated me from the raw realities of my childhood. I've managed to find eventual peace and healing. It took awhile, and I had a few setbacks, but I am closer now to wholeness than brokenness. My brothers, for multiple reasons, have not.

In closing, let's review the answer to the abiding question that sparked this book series: Why am I a healthy productive adult, when others, like my brothers, who had the same abusive childhood, are not? It's a fair question, but one without an easy answer.

There's not just one thing; it is a good deal more complex than that. After going through the process of writing my story, I can now put it down into ten clear points. These factors could be the basis for sound public policy and ministry priorities.

1. In the womb, I was protected by the state from permanent harm my mother could have done to me.

    Children exposed to alcohol and drugs in the womb can enter this world with irreversible damage. Yet child maltreatment legislation does not extend protection to children in utero. Pro-life efforts should include protecting the health, and not just the life, of the unborn.

2. For the critical first two years, I received proper care and nurture from my foster parents.

    Those early "plastic" years are fundamentally vital to the long-term physical health and emotional well-being of children. Early childhood intervention is paramount in our endeavors to raise successful children. The earlier we intervene in the life of a vulnerable child, the better off we'll all be.

3. The trauma was limited because I didn't live continually with my unstable mother.

    Removing children from their homes and separating them from their families is unquestionably harmful, but leaving them there may be as well. The type of care (residential facilities or foster families) is not as salient as the quality of care they receive. The goal is permanency in the most natural environment as possible. Reunification should be the first priority, but it should never be the only option.

4. Surrogate families and adult mentors, mostly from the Church, filled the gap in my life.

    The value of a well-run children's ministry through a local congregation is beyond measure. The eternal return on investment in incalculable. Local churches, denominational leaders, and parachurch groups must double, and even triple, their efforts if we are ever going to see the needle move in this area. Remember, commitment precedes resources.

5. I became a follower of Christ.

Studies continue to demonstrate the varied personal and social benefits of religious faith and practice. In ever increasingly secular societies, these benefits are, at best, ignored. Nonetheless, it's wise to have social policy that encourages faith communities to flourish, rather than burden them with regulations and bureaucracy when they try to help someone.

On a personal level, the gospel is the prescription for what ails us. Following Jesus, not simply practicing religion, is central to the entire healing process. Along with salvation comes a new template for processing all thoughts, attitudes, and actions. If heaven is the reward for *believing* in Jesus, a new life is the benefit of *following* Jesus.

6. Moving around so much actually gave me a larger view of the world and a longing for more in life.

In this regard, our young require two things. First, they need interaction with different people, cultures, and places. They need to experience life outside the confines of their family and community. Secondly, they must develop the ability to interpret those experiences through the truth-filter of biblical Christianity. Otherwise, they may be tempted to exchange one set of broken beliefs and failed ideas for another, leaving them with no better outcome.

7. I have never used drugs or alcohol.

Nothing has caused more harm to children, destroyed the lives of more adults, devastated more families, and wasted more valuable resources than drugs and alcohol. While the impact of the War on Drugs is questionable, there is little doubt in my mind that the move to a more open and tolerant policy will be even more devastating.

8. Education.

"Knowledge is power." "Education is the key." "A mind is a terrible thing to waste." Those are nice mottos, and they are true. Unfortunately, slick slogans are no substitute for effective education policy. We have allowed certain interest groups to turn our schools into venues for solving every social injustice and problem, rather than focusing on giving our children a good education—the one commodity that can actually solve all our other problems. Providing free lunches feeds hungry children. That's good. Teaching children to learn, then providing them useful knowledge, will prevent their children from being hungry. That's even better.

9. I married well.

As the family goes, so goes the society. As the marriage goes, so goes the family. Healthy marriages are essential to strong families, which, of course, are crucial for the success of children. We need to get back to promoting marriage and helping our children learn how to marry well. We need to teach them how to find a person they can happily spend the rest of their lives with and raise a family. In many ways, it's the first step to fixing the entire problem.

10. A life of serving others

A life of serving others has been therapeutic, as well as providing purpose to my past.

Nothing gives meaning and purpose to life like helping others. An entire book could probably be written on the subject. In short, healing our hurt often comes when we help to heal the hurts of others. The act of service is as much spiritual discipline as prayer or fasting. It's a unique way to get in touch with the divine.

From a thirty-thousand foot perspective, I suffered poverty and trauma for the first twenty years of my life. It took the next thirty years to be healed and made whole. The healing process is a marathon, not a sprint. I don't say that to discourage anyone—just the opposite. It's about having proper expectations. Those working towards resolution need to be realistic about the process and commit themselves to the long, and sometimes arduous, journey.

What's next for me? I am praying the remaining twenty to thirty years I may have left, Lord willing, be productive Kingdom work that focuses on rescuing and restoring vulnerable children and distressed families. I cannot think of any greater joy, or better purpose, for the rest of my life. For me, anything else is a colossal waste of time and energy.

Bottom Line: Deep inside each and every one of us is a terrible rot. Acting against our own rotten nature is evidence we have been truly redeemed.

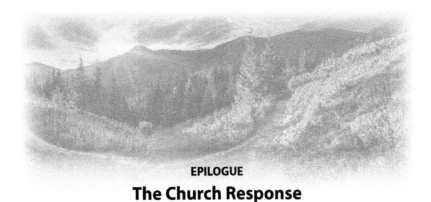

The Church Response

Fallen cultures produce broken families and weak communities,
which in turn harvest vulnerable children.

I SPENT THE LAST REMAINING MINUTES of 2013 as I usually did, in front of the television with my family watching the various New Year's Eve shows. Long gone are the days of Guy Lombardo or even Dick Clark helping us count down the minutes, waiting for the ball to drop in Times Square. As we channel surfed back and forth between the competing networks looking for something my wife and I could relate to, I grew more and more aggravated by what I was seeing and hearing.

It wasn't just a matter of taste. My four children helped me keep up with the times. What disturbed me was the crude and sexually implicit language, the idol worship of fans towards performers whose lifestyles, and shocking public acts, just seemed to get more brazen each year. I was perturbed by the smug, condescending comments of the host that revealed an elitist criticism of anything traditional or moral, not to mention the music that celebrated and promoted hedonism. It was just more than I could take, so we switched to a *Twilight Zone* marathon. After all, it felt like I was in another dimension and time.

The moment, however, that really stood out as a glaring demonstration of our rapidly declining social mores was a New Year's resolution from a random woman in the crowd. When a host of one of the shows asked a provocatively dressed young lady what her resolution for the New Year would be, she proudly proclaimed to the millions watching, "I'm going to get knocked up by my boyfriend."

That statement was unsettling on a number of levels. Beside the obvious fact she didn't seem to understand the nature of a resolution, the young party-goer demonstrated contempt for several moral standards. More importantly to our discussion here was her open attitude about her desired out-of-wedlock pregnancy. It was a perfect example of a social phenomenon known as the Durkheim Constant.

Bearing the name of the father of sociology, French philosopher Emile Durkheim first proposed the concept commonly known today as Defining Deviancy Down (a phrase first coined by the late Democratic Senator Patrick Moynihan). Some social scientists call it Social Entropy, referring to a lack of order of predictability—a gradual decline into disorder.

The theory suggests that there is a limit to the amount of deviant behavior any community can afford to recognize. As behavior worsens, the community's need to avoid ongoing conflict, coupled with its desire to maintain social equilibrium, will force it to adjust its moral and social standards downward so that conduct once thought shocking and disgraceful is gradually thought to be perfectly normal.

Let's think a minute about the young lady whose only goal for 2014 was getting pregnant by the guy she happened to like at the moment, or in her cheap view of it—"to get knocked up." Her goal was not engagement or marriage. It was not to buy a house and start a family with her husband, as generations past would have wanted. Her goal was to get pregnant outside the bounds and benefits of a committed marriage, and to expose her child to all the social problems clearly associated with young, single motherhood.

Some might think me unfair. Most likely she didn't wish any harm to come to her child. That's probably true. It's likely she was unaware of the problems statistically corresponding with her decision. Yet isn't that the point? Her predatory pregnancy had no forethought for the possibilities and outcomes. It would only be later when she had the child, but no longer had the boyfriend, that those things would become clear to her. By then it would be too late. The ramification of her selfish, thoughtless decision would long outlive her, and it would be the rest of us, you and me and our children, who would bear the price for her deviant decision.

I wonder if we are bearing that price now? I wonder if our tax dollars are supporting her and her toddler today?

---

544. We Need Them

I'm sure you're familiar with the term "Too Big to Fail." It's the belief of political leaders that there are some industries so vital to the economic well-being of our country that they cannot be allowed to go bankrupt. Some banks are too big to fail. The auto makers are too big to fail. I don't know about all that.

I am convinced, though, there is something in this country too small to fail, something too tiny to ignore: our children. All children come into this world the same — completely helpless. They are utterly weak and powerless. Their size, age, and immaturity (by that I mean lack of knowledge and experience) naturally make them easy targets for every social ill and human evil.

We cannot fail the children. They need our protection, guidance, focus, and resources. We cannot afford to allow them to be morally bankrupt, intellectually deficient, or emotionally damaged. Their well-being will determine the future of this nation, and that is too big to fail.

StraightTalkwithRobertDay.org

It's not that this type of thing didn't happen twenty or thirty years ago. It did. However, it happened in far fewer numbers, and when it did it wasn't celebrated as a major life accomplishment.

It was looked upon with some level of disappointment and, yes, even shame. There was a certain moral code in play that affected how society viewed unwed pregnancies, or premarital sex for that matter. It is the loss of shame that has partly helped speed up the Durkheim Constant.

In the name of tolerance, we have been fooled into believing that the highest moral standard today is to not offend someone. Community standards are slowly changing in order to embrace those who are formally outside the boundaries of convention. According to the Durkheim Constant, deviancy will continue to be redefined downward until it becomes normal and eventually even promoted as a value.

Robert Bork, in his 1997 book *Slouching Toward Gomorrah*, conjectured that the limits to deviant behavior actually expand in both directions, so that what was once deviant is not only considered normal, but what was moral is finally thought puritanical, or extremist, and in the name of tolerance, becomes irrelevant and even deviant. This reversed Durkheim Constant is called Defining Deviancy Up.

In other words, changing social mores go relentlessly in both directions. Mr. Bork summarized this problem well. He wrote, "So unrelenting is the assault on our sensibilities that many of us grow numb, finding resignation to be the rational, adaptive response to an environment that is increasingly polluted and apparently beyond our control."

I really like the way Kathleen Parker explained the Durkheim Constant. In an opinion piece she did for the *Washington Post* titled "Anthony Weiner and Defining Deviancy Down," she characterized it this way: "If you can't fix it, make it 'normal.'"

Divorce, pornography, unwed parenthood, sexting, whatever—it doesn't matter. As the number of those involved in such adverse behavior increases, and our ability to counter those behaviors decreases, we simply make those behaviors normal. That is the Durkheim Constant in a nutshell.

Are we at this state in our society because of the absence of a moral compass, or has humanity simply evolved to a more mature and tolerant mindset? The devil's advocate would argue that fifty years ago biracial marriages were considered immoral by conservative standards. Will we one day look back at homosexual relationships the way we looked at biracial relationships?

Everyone today, conservative or liberal, would say that our society has made great progress when it comes to women's rights. I can't think of any modern conservative who would argue that a woman doesn't have the right to vote, or shouldn't be paid as much as a man for the same job. Conservatives might disagree with liberals about the role of women in marriage and the family, but the point is that there is a general consensus that the role of women has changed in our society and that has mostly been a positive development.

So it could be said, at least in this case, that we have evolved to a more open and tolerant mindset. But let's now take on the very controversial issue of homosexuality. It is obvious that social attitudes are changing on this issue. It is now more open and certainly less stigmatized. Even conservatives are more tolerant about this issue than they were fifty years ago, and that is the point. The changing attitudes on homosexuality haven't changed because the moral truth that once governed this topic has changed, but because a growing number of people within our society has changed its mind about that moral truth. As that number grows, even those who still hold to that moral become less intolerant of the issue because of the social pressure that starts mounting.

Is this a fatalistic view? Will the Durkheim Constant always remain, always redefining what is right and wrong? Yes, left unchecked it will. But there is also good news. There have been times in history when the Durkheim Constant has been reset in a culture, a re-boot, if you will, of that culture's original moral standards. These are known as Spiritual Awakenings and Moral Revolutions.

We are seeing a reverse in the abortion debate, aren't we? That is one example of a specific moral issue where the Durkheim Constant is being held in check and actually going back in the other direction. The tide is turning to a more pro-life stance after years of pro-choice majority view and policy victories.

There also have been times in American history when there was an overhaul, society wide, in every category, a kind of shift back to traditional morals and values. There is nothing to say we cannot have that transpire today. If we can't, then the preaching of the gospel is in vain.

This constant will remain in society: changing standards until a movement of equal or greater force counters it. We will borrow a lesson from physics to explain: if there is no net force on an object, then its velocity is constant. The object is either at rest (if its velocity is equal to zero), or it moves with constant speed in a single direction.

Moral relativism is another major driving force behind the Durkheim Constant. Because moral relativism rejects notions of an absolute right or wrong in a given situation, everything is left for the individual to judge. Whatever the individual decides is then deemed acceptable. Those who object are accused of judging, and their idea of right and wrong is just as intolerant. If moral relativism goes unchecked, we will have anarchy and complete chaos.

Let's bring it closer to home. John Adams, the second president of the United States, said, "We have no government armed with power capable of contending with human passions unbridled by morality and religion. Avarice, ambition, revenge, or gallantry, would break the strongest cords of our Constitution as a whale goes through a net. Our Constitution was made only for a religious and moral people. It is wholly inadequate for the government of any other."

I think Adams may have understood the Durkheim Constant long before it was penned by Emile Durkheim. He and the other founders of our nation, and the framers of our Constitution, were keenly aware of the need for the nation to be built on absolute moral standards and a system of checks and balances. What they witnessed in their time from the French Revolution are the consequences of fallen natures, moral relativism, and defining deviancy down.

There is hope. I believe with all my heart that the social constant of defining deviancy both up and down can be stopped. It can even be reversed with a social movement of greater force. Biblical history shows that can happen, but not without a lot of work, perseverance, prayer, and even sacrifice.

If so, then we better get busy. There is too much at stake. Here's why.

Fallen cultures produce broken families and weak communities, which in turn harvest vulnerable children. Vulnerable children are easily overcome by the evils of humanity and become abused, neglected, abandoned, addicted, exploited, and eventually maladjusted. There's an enormous cost to society when those children grow up and become adults.

For the past several decades, our one country has become ever more divided into two nations. I'm not talking about politics. Sociologist James Q. Wilson best describes these two nations in a short article titled "Human Remedies for Social Disorders":

> In one nation, a child, raised by two parents, acquires an education, a job, a spouse, and a home kept separate from crime and disorder by distance, fences, or guards. In the other nation, a child is raised by an unwed girl, lives in a neighborhood filled with many sexual men but few committed fathers, and finds gang life to be necessary for self-protection and valuable for self-advancement. In the first nation, children look to the future and believe they control what place they will occupy in it; in the second, they live for the moment and think that fate,

not plans, will shape their lives. In both nations, harms occur, but in the second they proliferate—child abuse and drug abuse, gang violence and personal criminality, economic dependency and continued illegitimacy.

I grew up in the second nation—not in the inner cities now associated with the second nation but in poverty-stricken Appalachia. I didn't have to deal with the scourge of gangs, but every other description above applied to me, my family, and almost everyone else I knew.

For the longest time the second nation (rural and urban) has been the main breeding ground for vulnerable, distressed, and traumatized children. It's been the second nation that has performed the lion's share of harm to children. And those children grow up only to continue the destructive cycle. The surprising thing is that the first nation is quickly catching up to the second. We are witnessing today the unprecedented undoing of the first nation.

The first nation is now experiencing the same ratio of broken families as the second, but up to more recent times, their prosperity has largely shielded them from the same consequences. What is now overwhelming the advantages of their prosperity is the caustic influence of our fallen culture. In fact, their privileged circumstances may be speeding it along because their prosperity provides more access to the poisonous pop culture.

The bottom line is that our whole society is in trouble. The tidal wave of hedonism now washing over this country is destroying the basic foundations of our culture. It is destroying families and doing a great deal of harm to children. I know this from personal experience. I also know this from professional observation.

Something has to change. Something has to happen to turn this around for all of our sakes. But our hope will not be found in some kind of big, dramatic solution, and we cannot wait for someone else to fix it. There is no grand plan or noble leader that can, or will, save us from ourselves. The citizenry must take control of their own fate.

Cultures change for better or worse, Wilson reminds us, out of the countless small choices of millions of people; every citizen matters and it matters what every citizen decides. We will only restore this culture one decision at a time. It has to be done retail, not wholesale; person by person, family by family, community by community. More tax money for more government programs is not the answer. Congress cannot pass a law, no matter how comprehensive, that will repair it. While leadership is important, it will not matter what party is in power or the name of the person occupying the Oval Office.

Governments are good at transferring money, but not so good at transforming people. They can build solid bureaucracies, but they can't build strong families. They can subsidize a family, but they have yet to find a good substitute for it.

It's going to take a massive infusion of common sense and Christian principles into the cultural bloodstream to get it turned around. It's like fighting cancer. The cure will only come by restoring cell by cell until the entire body is healthy once again. That's where the Church comes in, doing what only the Church can do: change lives by changing hearts. We change hearts by changing minds (see Appendix A).

The culture has been in a death spiral for the past five decades. If we don't turn it around soon, the coming calamity may very well doom our nation to the trash heap of history. No longer is it acceptable for the Church to simply minister to the casualties of the culture wars—we must prevent the injury from occurring in the first place.

A World with a View

NATIONS, LIKE PEOPLE, LIVE AND DIE on their principles, even if they can't identify those principles — especially if they can't identify those principles. Many in America today bemoan the lack of principles in our society. In reality, though, it's not an absence of principles that is corrupting our society, but rather the prevalence of the wrong kind of principles.

Just to clarify, values are different from principles. Principles are those things we believe strongly. They are the doctrines of our lives. Values, then, are what flow naturally from our principles.

Principles produce values.

Values produce behaviors.

Behaviors, any and all behaviors, are really just the evidence of a set of principles that have been adopted. So when we talk about the decline of certain kinds of social behavior, or the increase of certain kinds of social deviancy, it isn't the lack of values that is to blame. What we are witnessing instead is the rise of a different set of values influencing those changes. We must go a step or two further than that, though, to really understand what is happening.

If behaviors are determined by values and values are birthed by principles, then where do principles come from? They don't just exist on their own in some sort of moral vacuum. No. Principles come from our fundamental beliefs (not necessarily from what we say we believe, but from what we really believe). Where then do beliefs come from? Well, beliefs come from a worldview that has some source of authority.

Worldview is the overall perspective from which one sees and interprets the world. Quite simply, it's a person's, or in the larger context, a society's view of the world. It is a collection of beliefs about life and the universe. Worldview is how individuals, or groups, or even nations, answer certain basic questions about life. Those questions can include:

How did we get here? It is the question of origin. Every religion tries to answer it.

What is wrong with us? It is the question about human behavior and the attempt to answer the question of evil.

How do we get fixed? Once the problem is identified, it is the goal of every religion to address how one is set free, corrected, or cured. It is the question of salvation.

Why are we here or, where are we going? It is the question about purpose and destiny. It's the meaning of life's questions we all ask ourselves at some point or other.

What is right and wrong? The question of ethics. Every society creates codes of law based on their answer to this question.

Think of worldview as a filter through which we interpret the universe we live in, or a pair of glasses tinted in some way that causes the wearer to see everything in that color. Worldview consists of the basic assumptions of life.

Take a piece of paper and a pen, and draw a line across the middle of the paper. Now draw a stick figure on top of the line, and beside the figure write the word Behavior.

(Stick figure here) Behavior

Now let's pick a behavior. For our purposes, let's use violence. The act of violence by that stick figure came from somewhere. My point is that all behavior, including violence, is not the result of a lack of values, or principles, but actually the result of a certain kind of values and principles.

That act of violence from the stick figure on your piece of paper could have been brought on by any number of values. The function of their reproductive organs, the melanin content of their skin, their facial feature or hair texture had nothing to do with it. The violence committed by that stick figure came from something unseen, but very real—values.

Those values we will place below the line. So write the word Values below the line. Values are below the line because they are underneath the surface, so to speak, but they become very public and visible to all when opportunity (in comparison with the strength of the value held) presents itself to the individual.

(Stick figure here) Behavior—violence
Values—prejudice

The violence of our stick figure could come from a number of values, but let's say that this particular act of violence came from a strongly held value of prejudice. Our stick figure has strong prejudicial feelings, and those feelings finally overflowed into a violent act toward another person. To prevent this from happening again, the stick figure would have to change the motivational value system. Society may punish that behavior. It may find ways to deter it. Yet the tendency will remain if the values remain.

Since behaviors are the result of values, where do values come from? On your piece of paper write the word Principles below the word value because it rests deeper down in the soil of our worldview.

(Stick figure here) Behavior—violence
Values—prejudice
Principles—racism

The value of prejudice felt so strongly by the stick figure was most likely influenced by a set of principles. One of those principles could be described as the "survival of the fittest." A person holding to this principle is convinced that the highest standard of human interest is self-interest. This principle might be described as "do unto others before they have a chance to do unto you." Or, the stick figure believes that his "people" (however that is defined) are naturally superior to other "peoples." The race of the stick figure is thought to be more advanced, blessed, or worthy than those of different races. These two principles combined is called racism.

However, principles, or what I called earlier the doctrines of our lives, come from somewhere too. They come from our beliefs. Now below the word principle on your piece of paper write the word Beliefs. Here we might be tempted to say that the stick figure believes in racism, and while his actions showed that to be true, racism is really a principle. The Theory of Evolution may be the belief system personally owned by our stick figure.

(Stick figure here) Behavior — violence
Values — prejudice
Principles — racism
Beliefs — evolution

Just to clarify, the doctrine of racism can be influenced by a number of sources, including religion and science. The theory of evolution was, at least, partially responsible for the extermination of six million Jews and other minorities in Nazi Germany. Certainly racism, and prejudice, and hate, can come from other belief systems, including religious beliefs, but our example here is a good one because we have historical evidence that it can also come from scientific beliefs, or at least what is thought to be the settled science of the day.

(Stick figure here) Behavior — violence
Values — prejudice
Principles — racism

Beliefs — evolution

Authority — faulty scientific theory

Now on your piece of paper, underneath the line, in big bold letters write the word Authority. All beliefs, great or small, have a source of authority. Beliefs, principles, and values, which eventually break through the line into reality, into the behaviors of our stick figure (and into our own lives), originate from some source of authority. It can be a book, a person, a tradition, an object, a scientific theory, a demon, or an angel — it doesn't really matter. The source of authority is where every person, and thus every society, develops its worldview.

Everything below the line can be described as worldview. It is what your stick figure is standing on. It is what your stick figure is using to interpret everything above the line. It is the source of all behaviors above that line. The stick figure may not be able to articulate any of it; nonetheless, it's still there.

Here's my point: those leading our society, social elites like educational leaders, politicians, and media moguls, understand that to change a nation's behavior is to first change that nation's deeply held beliefs. The culture wars we have been fighting in this country for the past four decades are really battles over systems of beliefs, not just a set of behaviors. While it is the behaviors we see, it's the consequences of those beliefs we encounter and deal with on a daily basis. Behaviors come with some kind of social and financial costs.

Bottom line: ideas have consequences.

Reality is what we make it because reality is the fruit of our beliefs. I believe all problems in American society today can be traced back to a faulty theology, in other words, a faulty belief system — the way we think about God, the world, and ourselves and others. The biblical admonition to be "transformed by the renewing of your mind" is not simply a personal call, it's also a cultural mandate.

We would probably all agree that if we wanted to change a person's behavior we would first have to change that person's thinking. The very same holds true for a society. If we want to change a society's behavior we first must change that society's thinking. We must change its mind, the way it views the world. We must change worldview if we want to do prevention, to keep individuals from being harmed. If we don't, we are doomed to forever just treat the casualties of the ancient struggle.

The enemies of Christianity, filled with the anti-Christ spirit, are working very hard to fundamentally transform our society by destroying the doctrines of Christianity, which are the foundations of our culture and society. They do it by attacking the validity of our source of authority, the Bible. We in the church, who are the guardians of those doctrines, must work equally hard to defend and promote them, or we will soon all be living in a world with a dramatically different view with all its corresponding behaviors.

Change Your Thinking, Change Your Life

"You are what you eat." Remember that slogan from your elementary school days? It makes complete sense from a biological standpoint. How much more true, then, is the saying, "You are what you think." Ralph Waldo Emerson said, "We become what we think about all day long." This is a disturbing concept when you consider the kinds of things our young people are spending all day thinking about. Junk in. Junk out.

When children are in a difficult situation or negative environment, we who love and care for them are quick to want to change their circumstances and get them out of that environment. However, we have got to understand that simply changing a child's circumstances alone does not change their life. A new environment, a different set of parents, better activities, a healthier diet, nicer clothes, a positive peer group, or more structure does not result in real or lasting change. Certainly, all these things are helpful, important, and needful, but none of these things will change the child or the family in the long term if we do not change their thinking.

Only lasting results are worth our efforts. Nothing short of a changed life is acceptable. Otherwise we are wasting our time. We can't merely treat the problem—we must fix the problem.

We have learned in our five decades of working with children and families at Patrick Henry Family Services that changing the outside does not change the inside. It never has, and it never will. Conversely, changing the inside always changes the outside. If we can change the way someone thinks, we can change the way they live. It's simple really. Bad thinking leads to bad fruit—that is behavior, decisions, circumstances. Good thinking, on the other hand, leads to good fruit.

Proverbs 23:7 declares, "As a man thinks in his heart so is he." According to this Scripture and a dozen or more like it in the Bible, a person is literally what he or she thinks. A person's character is the complete sum of all their thoughts. Their actions and behavior are the blossoms of their thoughts.

I am convinced that all problems (personal or corporate) are theological in nature. Change what people believe about God, themselves, the world, and others and you change the trajectory of their lives. The source of the following is unknown, but it speaks volumes to those open to knowing.

When you change your beliefs, you change your thinking;
When you change your thinking, you change your expectations;
When you change your expectations, you change your attitude;
When you change your attitude, you change your behavior;
When you change your behavior, you change your life.

Romans 1:1-2 tells us that transformation (change) comes by the "renewing of the mind." In short, what we do at Patrick Henry Family Services is a battle *of* and *for* the mind. Whether we are doing the ministry of camp, counseling, or child care, we understand it is essentially an ongoing struggle with our clients over which ideas they will embrace and live out.

Family Pictures

Robert Day and Karen Haynes were engaged in the winter of 1982. They met while attending Cumberland College in Williamsburg, Kentucky. Karen grew up in Southwest Alaska, but came to school in Kentucky because of her love of horses. Both Robert and Karen graduated from Cumberland College in 1984.

Alec Day, born September 1, 1986, riding on the shoulders of his dad. The Days were living then in Al Cordosa Trailer Park in Louisville, Kentucky. Robert was attending The Southern Baptist Theological Seminary where he earned a degree in Social Work. His childhood dream of living in a new mobile home in a trailer park with paved streets came true.

Robert Day's third brother, Randy Brown, had a winsome personality, but a troubled life. He died of unknown circumstances in spring of 2016.

The photograph above was taken in the summer of 1995 where Robert was serving as the full-time Senior Pastor for Alliance Bible Church, Anchorage, Alaska.

In the spring of 1997, Robert and Karen surrounded by their children sang for the congregation at Alliance Bible Church.

It was a meaningful ceremony for Karen and Robert as they renewed their vows while Robert was pastoring at First Baptist Church in Ketchikan, Alaska. Three of their four children were their attendants. (Sharon Day was not born at that time.)

After moving to Newcomb, Tennessee, Robert and Karen with their family made several efforts to reconnect with his mother, Cora Wendel. Cora and Richard Wendel lived in Pioneer, Tennessee.

*1998 photograph of Robert, centered, with his four half-brothers:
Leslie, Randy, David, and Joe Brown.*

Robert and the children enjoying a fun afternoon at the local park in the fall of 1998. The Days returned to Louisville, Kentucky, while Robert earned his Master of Divinity degree from The Southern Baptist Theological Seminary.

The Day family blackberry picking in the hills of Tennessee in July 1999.

Naomi, Faith, Robert, Sharon, and Alec in the fall of 2000.
Robert was serving as a full-time pastor of his home church,
Newcomb Baptist in Newcomb, Tennessee.

While on the way home from a family vacation in Washington, D.C., the Days stopped in Virginia's Shenandoah Valley. Robert remembers his wife saying, "Wouldn't it be nice if we lived in Virginia one day?"

The Days fostered baby Richie for twelve months. Richie is photographed above in December 2004 at seven months.

In 2006, the Days traveled back to Alaska for a family vacation which included their foster daughter, Michelle. Photographed at Kathleen Lake, Yukon, are Evan, Marjorie (Karen's parents), Naomi, Michelle, Faith, Robert, Karen, Alec, and Missy (Alec's wife).

SPREADING SOME SONSHINE

News Journal - October 31, 2007

SONday Enterprises started in May of 2007, by Perry Sears, co-owner with wife, Judy, of the SONshine Christian Store in Corbin, and Robert Day. Co-owner with wife, Karen, of Daylight Books, an e-commerce book company of Williamsburg. "SONshine" and "DAYlight"...thus, "SONday"! SONday Enterprises currently employees 17 individuals, 9 full-time and 8 part-time. They currently have over 280,000 books in stock. SONday Enterprises, LLC, in Williamsburg, held its ribbon cutting ceremony recently

The company is a world-wide wholesale distributor of quality, wholesome and inspiring books and educational materials representing numerous publishers. SONday sells retail for fundraising through book fairs in schools, churches and other organizations nationwide. This division is called "Books for Funds" and has as its motto: "Fill their minds, Feed their souls, Fund your program." Sponsoring schools or organizations receive a substantial portion of the revenue from the book fairs. It is located at 1059 N. Hwy 25W, Williamsburg. Business phone numbers are: 888-539-9464, 606-539-9464, and fax: 606-539-9472. Pictured above are: Carolyn Massengill, Stacie Evans, Eva Jane Smith, Josh Bunch, Michael Sawyers, Roddy Harrison, Pat White, Jr. Karen Day, Robert Day, Noah Preston, Sharon Rose Day, Perry Sears, Judy Sears, Becky Bargo, Kay Swartz, Paul Steely. Back row- Stella Steely, Blane Stewart, Carolyn Stewart, Drew Preston, Colby Wilson, Joe Smitty, Denny Kell, Luke Preston, Tammy Preston, and Ida Stallcup.

Photos by DEBRA WRIGHT

In 2007, Robert, co-owner, opened a wholesale book business in Williamsburg, Kentucky. His life-long friend, Drew Preston (in the lower left corner), joined the team. Unhappily, due to the economy's crash in 2008, the business closed within a year.

Karen and Robert Day walking on the beach at Lake Michigan in 2009. Robert enjoys telling friends, "When you marry well, you eventually even walk alike!"

It was a special reunion for Robert when Aunt Moe came to visit him in the summer of 2012. They are photographed above at Red Hill, the burial site of Patrick Henry.

Robert Day with his wife, Karen, and their four children,
Faith, Naomi, Sharon, and Alec, in Goshen, Indiana.

About the Author
ROBERT J. DAY
MSW, MDV

Married
Father of 4
CEO of Patrick Henry Family Services
Broadcast Host of Straight Talk
Author

Born to an unwed, teenaged mother, Robert's childhood of poverty and abuse included more than 35 temporary homes before his unlikely graduation from high school. Today, through God's grace, and with two Masters degrees in hand, Robert's life work is dedicated to keeping children safe and families strong. As CEO of Patrick Henry Family Services, Robert is successfully leading the organization to the forefront in the child welfare industry. His vision and leadership for a revolution in residential care and counseling have proven effective. Robert has also built a strong following as the host of Straight Talk, a popular, daily broadcast. His moving, inspiring testimony, together with his unique and timely perspective, has made Robert Day a sought after speaker for conferences, churches, civic audiences and beyond.

robertjdayauthor.org I patrickhenry.org

Straight Talk with Robert J. Day

...a broadcast ministry of Patrick Henry Family Services

Uplifting and encouraging messages on some of the most challenging issues facing families today.

THE BEST TIME TO PLANT A TREE

IS TWENTY YEARS AGO

There's a tree in my yard that bends. As it grows, it will eventually break under its own weight. It's inevitable, and that's a shame. I like the tree. It's in a good spot and provides needed shade. When it comes down, it will take years to replace, probably more years than I have left to live.

There's an old Chinese proverb which speaks to the need of every parent to teach their children early: "The best time to plant a tree is twenty years ago." That reminds me of the biblical proverb, "Teach a child in the way they should go when they are young, when they are old they will not depart from it."

The best time to plant wisdom in the heart of my children was twenty years ago. They're adults now, and the direction of their life is pretty much set. It's a great deal more difficult to straighten them out now. They will either stand tall, or fall under their own weight.

Take away: A seedling will grow in whatever direction you set it.

Follow Straight Talk on Twitter and Facebook, or you can enjoy Straight Talk in both written and audio formats on straighttalkwithrobertday.org and patrickhenry.org.

...challenging the way we think and live!

IN NEED OF A SPEAKER FOR YOUR NEXT EVENT?

Now you can have *Robert J. Day* as keynote speaker
for your next conference, meeting or other event.

Check out the full team of dynamic speakers and presenters
from the Patrick Henry Family Services Speakers Bureau
at patrickhenry.org or by calling 434.376.2006

Patrick Henry Family Services

Speakers BUREAU

PATRICK HENRY
FAMILY SERVICES

Another book from
Patrick Henry Family Services Publishing

Get your copy of 'Straight Talk for the journey'; a devotional style book filled with uplifting, challenging and inspirational excerpts from the popular broadcast, Straight Talk with Robert Day.

Order your copy today at patrickhenry.org

Follow Straight Talk on Twitter and Facebook, or you can enjoy Straight Talk in both written and audio formats on straighttalkwithrobertday.org and patrickhenry.org.

Patrick Henry Family Services

Patrick Henry Family Services
is a faith-based, 501c3, non-profit
which has been serving the children, families and
communities of
Central Virginia since 1961.

Sustained entirely through donations,
Patrick Henry Boys and Girls Homes,
Hope for Tomorrow counseling,
Safe Families for Children,
Hat Creek Camps,
The Hammersley Center at Hat Creek,
Straight Talk Radio
and many other dynamic programs, all work together to accomplish the
mission of keeping children safe and families strong.

*To learn more, or to discover how you can be involved
with this vital ministry,
call us today at 434.376.2006, or go to patrickhenry.org.*

Now that you have read
'Desperately Healed...My Journey to Wholeness',
by Robert J. Day,
don't miss books 1 and 3 in this compelling series
'Rescuing Children...Healing Adults'.

Book 1:

'Worst of Mothers...
Best of Moms'

Order your copy today at
robertjdayauthor.org or amazon.com

Now that you have read
'Desperately Healed…My Journey to Wholeness',
by Robert J. Day,
don't miss books 1 and 3 in the series
'Rescuing Children…Healing Adults'.

Book 3

'Liberty or Death…
a Revolution in Child Welfare'

Available for pre-order at
robertjdayauthor.org or patrickhenry.org

Book 1 - *Worst of Mothers…Best of Moms*

Born to an unwed, teenage mother, his childhood of poverty, neglect and unspeakable abuse included more than 35 homes before his unlikely graduation from high school. Today, as CEO of Patrick Henry Family Services, Robert Day's life work is dedicated to keeping children safe and families strong. 'Worst of Mothers…Best of Moms', is a moving and inspirational story of hope and restoration, and provides a new perspective on the sovereignty of God.

Book 2 - *Desperately Healed…My Journey to Wholeness*

Surviving the kind of oppressive poverty, neglect and terrifying abuse Robert Day suffered as a child implores the question asked by so many; 'how did you get out…how did you find healing?' Childhood trauma leaves an intensely painful wound on the adult, long after the child is grown. In this, his second of a three-part series, Robert shares the emotions, mistakes and often excruciating steps necessary to find, and eventually embrace, that place of 'wholeness'.

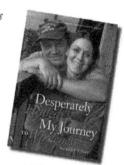

Book 3 - *Liberty or Death…Leading a Revolution in Child Welfare*

Grown, desperately healed and successfully leading a non-profit ministry in the child welfare industry, author Robert Day questions why preventable abuse still continues, as it did in his own story. This third and final book in the 'Rescuing Children…Healing Adults' series provides a painfully transparent look at how our broken culture and dysfunctional systems have treated the most helpless among us. But there is hope; through innovative, Christ-centered, common-sense approaches, the child welfare system and the church can remold history and revision the future to help keep children safe and restore shattered families…a revolution in child welfare.

Celebrating 10 years
of service to Central Virginia

Hope for Tomorrow Counseling provides caring, professional counseling services to children, adults, family and community. Serving Central Virginia since 2007, Hope for Tomorrow now has offices in:

BEDFORD * DANVILLE * FARMVILLE
LYNCHBURG * MIDLOTHIAN
SOUTH BOSTON * BROOKNEAL

Hope for Tomorrow Counseling is a ministry of Patrick Henry Family Services
hopefortomorrowcounseling.org